PRACTISING THE

ART OF
WRITING

FOR ADVANCED LEVEL ENGLISH

PATRICIA GORDON

Hodder & Stoughton

A MEMBER OF THE HODDER HEADLINE GROUP

Cataloguing in Publication Data is available from the British Library

ISBN 0 340 654619

First published 1996
Impression number   10 9 8 7 6 5 4 3 2 1
Year   1999 1998 1997 1996

Typeset by Transet Ltd, Coventry, England
Printed in Great Britain for Hodder & Stoughton Educational, a division of Hodder Headline Plc, 338 Euston Road, London NW1 3BH by Redwood Books, Trowbridge, Wiltshire.

Contents

Introduction for Teachers

This book is intended to help students with the different kinds of writing in English that they undertake for certificate and examination purposes. Although it is addressed directly to the students, encouraging their independence as writers, it clearly cannot replace the day-to-day work that you do in motivating, teaching, challenging and responding to their writing. Such teaching skills will give students the security and confidence to embark and continue on a process of development as writers that is inevitably gradual and long-term.

Throughout the book the importance of the relationship between writer and reader is seen as central. Established writers are used as models. There is a collection of complete texts in Section Two. The study of these, and the texts referred to on page 4, is seen as integral to the students' growing appreciation of the writer's craft. Your support in sustaining the students' engagement with these texts will be important. The texts in Section Two may also provide a modest resource for other aspects of teaching English.

Acknowledgements

The author and the publishers would like to thank the following authors and publishers for permission to reproduce copyright material:

Neal Ascherson and the *Independent on Sunday* for 'After the Freedom, Bread'

David Attenborough and HarperCollins for an extract from *Life on Earth*

William Boyd and Penguin for 'Not Yet, Jayette' from *On the Yankee Station*

Iain Crichton Smith and Canongate for an extract from *Consider the Lilies*

Alistair Cooke and Penguin for 'It's a Democracy, Isn't It?' from *Alistair Cooke's Letters from America 1946–1951*

Jonathan Cape for 'Stopping by Woods on a Snowy Evening' from *The Poetry of Robert Frost*, edited by Edward Connery Lathen

William Golding and Faber and Faber for extracts from *Lord of the Flies*

Penguin for an extract from Graham Greene's 'Jubilee' from *Twenty-One Stories*

The Estate of Ernest Hemingway for 'A Clean, Well-Lighted Place' from *Winner Takes Nothing* and Jonathan Cape for an extract from 'Cross-Country Snow' from *The Snows of Kilimanjaro*

Ted Hughes and Faber and Faber for an extract from *Poetry in the Making*

Victor Keegan and *The Guardian* for extracts from 'The Riviera Touch'

Margaret Laurence and Penguin for an extract from 'To Set Our House in Order' from *The Penguin Book of Canadian Short Stories*

Laurie Lee and Chatto and Windus for an extract from *Cider with Rosie*

Liz Lochhead and Reprographia for an extract from 'Revelation' from *Memo for Spring*

George Mackay Brown and John Murray (Publishers) Ltd. for 'The Bright Spade' from *A Time to Keep*

Bernard MacLaverty and The Blackstaff Press for 'Secrets' from *Secrets and Other Stories*

Brian McCabe and Mariscat for 'Comparisons' from *Spring's Witch* and Mainstream for an extract from 'Anima' from *The Lipstick Circus*

Andrew Marr and *Scotland on Sunday* for 'Strong Tonic for the Anaemic Body Politic'

Faber and Faber for an extract from 'The Good Town' in *Collected Poems* by Edwin Muir

Harold Pinter and Faber and Faber for 'Last to Go' and 'Request Stop' from *Pinter Plays: Two*

V. S. Pritchett and Chatto and Windus for an extract from 'The Key to My Heart' from *Collected Stories*

The Estate of Robertson Davies and Viking Penguin for an extract from *Murther and Walking Spirits*

William Sansom and The Hogarth Press for an extract from 'The Vertical Ladder' from *Stories*

Alan Sillitoe for an extract from 'On Saturday Afternoon' (© Alan Sillitoe 1959, 1987) from *The Loneliness of the Long-Distance Runner*

Muriel Spark and Macmillan for 'You Should Have Seen the Mess' from *The Go-Away Bird*

William Heinemann Ltd for an extract from *Of Mice and Men* by John Steinbeck

J. M. Dent for an extract from Dylan Thomas's 'Do Not Go Gentle into that Good Night'

Penguin for an extract from *Matilda's England* by William Trevor

John Updike and Penguin for an extract from 'A Sense of Shelter' from *Pigeon Feathers and Other Stories*

John Wells and the *Independent on Sunday* for 'Nice Work If You Can Define It' (© John Wells 1995)

Angus Boulton and the *Independent on Sunday* for the photograph on page 126.

■ *Section One* ■

Start Here

Listen to yourself thinking and you will hear the running conversation that you have with yourself. Perhaps when you wake up in the morning you start a monologue that goes something like this?

'What time is it? What day is it?

'Tuesday! Yes, Tuesday.

'Must remember to take the dog to the vet/
finish my Biology homework/
mow the grass/
collect the cleaning/
see the Guidance teacher'... And so on.

Consider the following type of monologue going on inside someone's head. (Sometimes these are even spoken aloud.)

'Now, there's just enough undercoat left for the door. What about the window? Can I manage without? Wait. There's a bit in a tin under the stair – That'll do...' And so on.

Why do we do this? Does it serve a purpose?

Yes it does. In some ways we write the book of our lives in our heads. We try to organise ourselves, gather thoughts, marshal ideas, categorise and file experiences, and plan events. But it isn't all functional: we also dream and hope and construct little interludes and playscripts; we re-invent ourselves; we define and re-define characters; we test out our ideas, feelings, prejudices; we rehearse our beliefs and arguments, our defences and attacks – and our lines of love! All inside our heads. We process our lives all the time. And we are constantly learning from this. And yet, when called upon to write even a small part of the kind of life that goes on inside our heads, we often feel inadequate, unmotivated, insecure, think that we have nothing to say, don't know how to start, cannot decide what to select. And so on. It seems a rather daunting and messy task – a little like clearing the attic.

Perhaps one of the most important aids to writing is to understand that there is a link between the thoughts inside our heads and what we write. We need to bring to the paper the uniqueness of ourselves – not view writing as something that is separate from self, belonging only to school.

It is hoped that this book will give you the confidence to free these thoughts, to allow you to shape and craft them. *All* writing imposes some kind of shape on the chaos that is experience, feelings, events, thoughts – life itself. This book is intended to help you to do justice to your ideas, feelings, experiences – to your own uniqueness – in creative writing of various kinds, which will carry your own individual voice.

In order to help you to do all this and to make the link between your inner voice and your written piece, try to think of yourself not only as a pupil having to write something for school (or examinations), but also as an apprentice writer who will, over a period of time, develop the skills of the craft. No learner finds immediate success, but being prepared to practise and try things out, and most important of all, learn from those who have mastered the art, will bring you confidence, help your progress, and be fun.

Mastery, of course, might never be achieved in a lifetime. But if you are prepared to make the commitment to your own development, to observe, to think, to listen – and, above all, to read – you should find the writer in yourself. Throughout the book, the relationship between reader and writer is emphasised, and you will find several texts to help you to explore it and to respond to suggestions to develop your own practice. As you work through the book you will also find suggestions and stimuli for writing and a variety of tasks to engage in. The tasks, which range from simple warm-up preparation for writing to producing complete pieces, are identified by the sign ■ .

It is hoped that not only will you become conscious of your own strengths and learn to develop them but that also, in looking closely at how established writers craft their work, you will come to appreciate the critical relationship between reader and writer and to appreciate the ways in which a writer works creatively with his or her material. Developing your skills and artistry in writing is a process that takes time. However, if you take responsibility for practising and improving your writing you will find that it can be fun.

The book is divided into two main sections, with an index. Section One contains a short chapter on preparation for writing and six further chapters, which look at the important elements in the craft of writing in a variety of genres, and present suggestions and opportunities for you to practise your skills in these. The chapters are punctuated with brief summaries so that you can keep a check on your progress. There is also a helpline chapter entitled

'A Second Opinion'. This is intended to give 'emergency' help and provide further lines of thought on work by authors that you are asked to consider. If help or hints are available these will be indicated in the main text.

Section Two contains a small collection of the writers' works that are referred to in Section One, a few photographs, and newspaper cuttings. Finally, there is an index.

Section One   Chapter 1 offers you encouragement in ways of approaching writing. Chapters 2 and 3 take a detailed look at narrative writing, in particular the short story. Narrative is the genre with which you are probably most familiar. The decision to make it the main focus of the book is intended to allow you to develop skills you have been practising for a long time – but it also recognises that these skills form an essential grounding for writing of all kinds. Chapter 4 begins with the monologue and then makes the link between this and the writing of drama. Chapter 5 considers the writing of poetry. Chapter 6 deals with personal writing. Chapter 7 looks at writing informational texts. There are activities throughout the chapters to help you to develop confidence and independence in your approach to writing and to lay foundations for what is a long-term process. In several instances the activities suggest working with a partner. If you do not happen to be working in the classroom you are advised to work with a friend so that you can experience the benefits of working in pairs.

A lot of what is said in Section One will be familiar to you, and should allow you to revise your understanding of the characteristics of the various genres. The first few activities are intended to limber you up and introduce you to ways of approaching writing that make it enjoyable. They should also help to build confidence. Throughout the section you will be asked to read and consider a variety of literary texts and short extracts from writers. These will all serve to provide you with models of writing which will help to establish your appreciation of the craft of the writer. Thus, you will be encouraged to consider the texts from the point of view of the *writer* as well as respond to the texts as a *reader* – something with which you are already familiar. As you work with the material, consult with your teacher about your progress – and, of course, about your pieces of writing.

Section Two   In addition to the texts that are included in this section it is assumed that you have read, or will read, the following:

FICTION

Lord of the Flies, William Golding (novel)
Of Mice and Men, John Steinbeck (short novel)
Consider the Lilies, Iain Crichton Smith (novel)
The Catcher in the Rye, J. D. Salinger (novel)
The Turn of the Screw, Henry James (long short story)
Odour of Chrysanthemums, D. H. Lawrence (short story)

POETRY

My Last Duchess, Robert Browning (dramatic monologue)
Telephone Conversation, Wole Soyinka
The Jaguar, Ted Hughes
Revelation, Liz Lochhead
Boundaries, Norman MacCaig
Inversnaid, G. M. Hopkins
Do Not Go Gentle into that Good Night, Dylan Thomas
Stopping by Woods on a Snowy Evening, Robert Frost

DRAMA

Pygmalion, George Bernard Shaw
and will have access to videotapes of *Fawlty Towers*, BBC

AUTOBIOGRAPHY

Cider with Rosie, Laurie Lee

1

Becoming a Writer

There are numerous ways in which we use writing to make sense of our lives. Many of these are simply concerned with helping us to organise ourselves. We write lists and notes of things to do or remember – both of which are concerned with classification or putting things into order. We also write little stories when we write messages (and, of course, in many of our letters).

> Mum says bring the washing in if it rains. She's going to Gran's after work and might be late. I'm going out to my pal's.

Here are some suggestions as to how you might help yourself to prepare for the kinds of writing which this book seeks to develop. You will need ideas, material for writing – and you will need to order and to shape your material. Finding ideas and gathering material requires, on your part, an active interest and engagement with the world around you, and with the imagination and the intellect. Rather like a painter, a writer needs to be observant: to look at, listen to and then to reflect on the life going on around and the people who are a part of it. When making the link between this and your inner life, your thoughts, observations, ideas, dreams and daydreams, it can be helpful to jot down notes of the things that occur to you, and the things that you observe. These can be collected: they are a resource.

Keep a note-pad beside the bed and get into the habit of jotting down your first and last thoughts – and dreams. Read these over at intervals. They will provide you with excellent stimulus and raw material for your writing. Another useful practice is to think up, and jot down when you find the opportunity, short biographies of people you see in crowds, on buses and trains. You might find it quite entertaining to think up nicknames for people you see or encounter – 'Mrs Misery', 'Tufty' – or short, descriptive phrases like 'Worried of Woking'. Training yourself to be observant in this way, and to let your imagination work on your observations, establishes some of the groundwork for characterisation.

You might consider trying to write mini-dramas of scenes you observe between people – perhaps in the park, in the street, whatever. Teach yourself to notice people's behaviour, to observe and recognise what is unfolding in front of you. This will also involve thinking about what motivates individual actions, and should help you to write convincing dramatic scenes and thoughtful characterisation as well as well-constructed narrative. Further preparation for characterisation can be made by careful and intelligent listening. Listen to the variety of ways in which people talk to each other (and to themselves). Listen to the tone of voice, the emotion in the voice, the changing rhythms of speech; and listen for the words not spoken.

What do we do with all this material – our collection of experiences, ideas and observations? When starting to write, one of the main challenges is to create order out of the haphazardness and chaos of our raw material – rather like pinning down our dreams. To attempt to create some kind of order so that we can communicate with the listener or reader, we have to feel, remember, select, discard, prune, polish, until we find the shape that we want.

If you are prepared to make a commitment to observing, listening, and thinking, you will provide yourself with ample material for writing. When you are called upon to write – to create something from almost nothing – this material will help you to make those vital connections between reality and imagination. Making these connections and then transforming them through the imagination is largely what writing is all about.

SUMMARY

- start to collect ideas for writing
- develop the habit of jotting down ideas and interesting fragments
- observe what is going on around you
- think about what motivates behaviour
- listen to the things people say

2

Narrative Writing:
the opening and the viewpoint

We shall start with narrative writing because it is the most familiar and often the apprentice writer's first choice – and because, in many of its characteristics, it gives us the basis of most of our writing. You have, no doubt, been writing stories since early primary school and *telling* stories long before that. Much writing (even when it is not fiction) carries a narrative shape. You will find such a shape in drama and in journalism – note the journalist's reference to 'the story' – as well as in story-writing itself.

We are all story-tellers. Every anecdote, every joke, every piece of gossip, each recounting of something that has happened, we make into a story. Our dreams and nightmares are stories which, when retelling, we sometimes find difficult to put into logical shape (because dreams, of course, have no clear logic). Our thoughts and hopes and daydreams are stories. A lot of our thinking has a narrative structure; many of our memories have a narrative form, and thoughts about the future are often projected through narrative. Indeed, many of our experiences we shape into narratives in order to make sense of them and remember them. We give history a narrative, as well as a chronological, shape because narrative is concerned with making connections, not just cause and effect. These connections are not only logical, they are also emotional and psychological.

When we tell stories, anecdotes and jokes we attempt to shape them to create an effect, make an impact, raise a laugh. If we can do these things, or some of these things, when we *tell* stories we can, by a similar process, *write* stories. You are probably aware of how stories, anecdotes and jokes improve with the telling. Instinctively (and, of course, depending on audience feedback), the teller is fine-tuning his or her act! In just the same way when we write we need to fine-tune the text until we are satisfied with the finished piece.

- Think about telling an anecdote or a piece of gossip. Remember the last joke you told. Go over it carefully. Write it down. Now give it to your partner to read. Did you manage to attract his or her attention? If so, how did you do it?

Here are the first challenges of story-telling:

> to grab the reader's attention
> to set up expectations and a sense of anticipation in the reader
> to invite the reader into the world of the story and to make him or her want to share its adventures and experiences and to get to know the people who inhabit that world.

■ THE BEGINNING

Grabbing the reader's attention means that we have to *begin well*. There are many ways in which writers begin their stories, but the intention is always to open the door and invite the reader in ... *Once upon a time*... But there is more to be considered than just inviting the reader in. The writer has to create not only a need-to-turn-the-page factor for the reader but also to establish in the text a number of signals that will suggest to the reader something of the complexity and detail to follow. And the writer must do all this without baffling the reader or making everything that takes place tediously obvious.

- Just for a few minutes think up, and write down, four opening sentences that will immediately attract the reader. Show these to a partner and discuss the expectations set up by the opening, both those set up in your partner, and those you had intended to set up. Is there any correspondence?

When writing a story it is worth remembering that it has a larger life than the episodes written on the page. This is particularly true of the opening. The people and places existed before the story starts, and continue to exist after it finishes. As story-tellers, therefore, we have to decide **when, where** and **how** to invite the reader in. In many ways the story is like a painting that remains hidden, until the writer chooses to reveal it. And only a little at a time will be revealed. The critical question is always which bit will the writer reveal first? What clues will the writer give us from the first moment to allow us to start to guess at the whole picture? Experiment with opening sentences – they are little puzzles or mysteries which the reader wants to solve. They also help you, the writer, to move your story along, because a beginning means that there is a tale waiting to be told.

You will perhaps have been told that when writing a story it is important to set the scene. Very often the apprentice writer will think that this calls for a descriptive opening, like a theatre backdrop awaiting the entry of the main character. This is a little like writing by numbers. Remember, your opening is not determined by rules, but by what you want to do. You might want to start at the 'end' of the story, as it were. You might wish immediately to share with the reader some insight into character(s) and so start with dialogue. You might wish to start with an incident that is crucial to the story. You might wish to focus on something symbolic, right at the outset. You might decide to start with an enigma intended to tantalise the reader. You could start at a crisis point, or, alternatively, start quietly and build up towards a crisis. You might decide to have a one-word scene-setter, for example: *Monday*.

■   Here is a selection of narrative openings. Read them, and after you have read each one, take a minute or two to jot down your first responses. For instance:

> what does it make you think or feel?
> what puzzles you?
> what do you want to find out?
> what captured your attention?
> what expectations have been aroused in you?
> In short, what first impressions has the story made on you?

■   When you have done this, compare your jottings with a partner. Do you find similarities? Discuss and justify the differences you find.

1 'Hurry up and make up yer mind,' said my father.

I went on staring at the dinette linoleum in silence. It wasn't yellow and it wasn't quite brown, but a sort of diarrhoea-colour in between. It was making me feel queasy, staring at it like this. I remembered my sister telling me that its pattern was called parquet and that it was just like Mum to buy lino that pretended to be wood. What had she meant by that? And what had she meant when she'd said that a dinette wasn't the same as a dining room? What was the difference? And why did we call it the dinette anyway? Nobody ate in here. Everybody ate in the living room, with the telly on and the fire. The only thing anyone ever did in the dinette was sulk. That was what it was for.

2 Mr Chalfont ironed his trousers and his tie. Then he folded up his ironing-board and put it away. He was tall and he had preserved his figure: he looked distinguished even in his pants, in the small furnished bed-sitting-room he kept off Shepherd's Market. He was fifty, but he didn't look more than forty-five.

3 When Father dropped dead and Mother and I were left to run the business on our own, I was twenty-four years old. It was the principal bakery in our town, a good little business, and Father had built it up from nothing. Father used to wink at me when Mother talked about their 'first wedding'. 'How many times have you been married? Who was it that time?' he used to say to her. She was speaking of the time they first ventured out of the bakery into catering for weddings and local dances.

4 I was never so amazed in my life as when the Sniffer drew his concealed weapon from its case and struck me to the ground, stone dead.

How did I know that I was dead? As it seemed to me, I recovered consciousness in an instant after the blow, and heard the Sniffer saying, in a quavering voice: 'He's dead! My God, I've killed him!' My wife was kneeling by my side, feeling my pulse, her ear to my heart; she said, with what I thought was remarkable self-possession in the circumstances, 'Yes, you've killed him.'

5 Snow fell against the high school all day, wet big-flaked snow that did not accumulate well. Sharpening two pencils, William looked down on a parking lot that was a blackboard in reverse; car tyres had cut smooth arcs of black into the white, and wherever a school bus had backed around, it had left an autocratic signature of two V's.

6 When the baby was almost ready to be born, something went wrong and my mother had to go into hospital two weeks before the expected time. I was wakened by her crying in the night, and then I heard my father's footsteps as he went downstairs to phone. I stood in the doorway of my room shivering and listening, wanting to go to my mother but afraid to go lest there be some sight there more terrifying than I could bear.

7 I once saw a bloke try to kill himself. I'll never forget the day because I was sitting in the house on a Saturday afternoon, feeling black and fed up because everybody in the family had gone to the pictures, except me who'd for some reason been left out of it. 'Course, I didn't know then that I would soon see something you can never see in the same way on the pictures, a real bloke stringing himself up. I was only a kid at the time, so you can imagine how much I enjoyed it.

8 As he felt the first watery eggs of sweat moistening the palms of his hands, as with every rung higher his body seemed to weigh more heavily, this young man Flegg regretted in sudden desperation, but still in vain, the irresponsible events that had thrust him up into his present precarious climb. Here he was, isolated on a vertical iron ladder flat to the side of a gasometer and bound to climb higher and higher until he should reach the vertiginous skyward summit.

9 There was once a King, and he had a Queen, and he was the manliest of his sex, and she was the loveliest of hers. The King was, in his private profession, Under Government. The Queen's father had been a medical man out of town.

They had nineteen children, and were always having more. Seventeen of these children took care of the baby, and Alicia, the eldest, took care of them all. Their ages varied from seven years to seven months.

Let us now resume our story.

10 The funicular car bucked once more and then stopped. It could not go farther, the snow drifted solidly across the track. The gale scouring the exposed surface of the mountain had swept the snow surface into a wind-board crust. Nick, waxing his skis in the baggage car, pushed his boots into the toe irons and shut the clamp tight. He jumped from the car sideways on to the hard wind-board, made a jump turn, and crouching and trailing his sticks slipped in a rush down the slope.

And, of course, one of the most famous opening sentences is found in George Orwell's novel *Nineteen Eighty-Four*:

It was a bright cold day in April, and the clocks were striking thirteen.

Sometimes a writer can take the reader right into a story with the skill and simplicity of only one sentence – as in the opening sentence of George Mackay Brown's short story *The Bright Spade* (see Section Two, page 66):

That winter the gravedigger was the busiest man in the island.

Such economy contributes to the impact made on the reader. And it is important to remember that a short story needs to make its impact as economically as possible. The writer makes everything count; everything works towards the complete whole. In establishing a character, for instance, each little piece should build up the reader's picture and understanding. This is unlikely to be complete at first: each reading will put the pieces, the clues, together more securely.

■ Look at extract 10 and note the economy with which setting, introduction of character, narrative viewpoint, mood and episode are being established in this first paragraph. This is a very 'clean' opening to a story – but it is neither obvious nor predictable.

■ Working in pairs, look carefully at extract 1. What is your response to it? What clues to the whole picture has the writer given you? Pay attention to the detail. The following suggestions should guide you.

You might think about the contrast between the father's opening words and the narrator's inner voice – and what this tells us about each of them.
What do we find out about the mother and the sister from the narrator's thoughts?
What do we learn about the family from the little details?
What does the list of questions suggest to us about the narrator?
Can you imagine what might have happened before the story starts?
What might happen next?

From your notes, you will find that you have begun to build up a picture of the characters, although you are puzzled about what has happened before and what might happen next. It seems, then, that in this example, the author lets us little by little into the narrative by way of the characters – particularly the central narrative voice – which are presented both through speech and through internal monologue.

■ Refer to your notes and consider the important characteristics of a story (not all of them, of course, can be demonstrated in the opening) and how these apply to this particular short story. (These characteristics will be considered at other points in this book.)

where is the story set? when is it taking place? }	setting
who is/are the main character/s?	characterisation
who is telling the story?	narrative viewpoint
what signs are there as to what will happen in the story?	plot and development
what atmosphere/s is/are created?	mood and tone
how does it end?	ending/dénouement

■ Look at extract 2. Again, look for the clues the writer gives. Discuss these with your partner, and what the writer could do next. Now write the next paragraph, taking care to maintain the mood of the opening. See note 1, page 63.

■ Consider extract 9. How do you respond to the opening of this fairy tale, *The Magic Fish-Bone* by Charles Dickens? Have your expectations of the genre been met? Is Dickens's treatment of the genre humorous? If so, how is the humour achieved?

■ THE NARRATIVE VIEWPOINT

It can be helpful when thinking about narrative viewpoint to connect it to cinematic technique. On film the viewpoint is quickly and visibly established by the position of the camera. For instance, if the central character, whose 'story' the viewer is following, enters a room with other people in it, has a blazing row with someone and then leaves the room, the camera leaves with him. If the camera remains in the room (or returns to the room) to focus on the responses of the other people, this would indicate a shift in viewpoint from the 'hero' to other characters.

Roughly speaking, you can adopt one of the following stances – or viewpoints – when writing narrative:

the omniscient narrator
the 'straight' narrator

the third person from one particular character's point of view
the first person (who inevitably 'filters' the narrative)
a sequence of third person viewpoints
a sequence of first person viewpoints

The omniscient narrator knows everything that happens (off stage as well as on, as it were), knows what each character thinks and feels. This narrator is in control of the reader and will determine what is revealed and when. (Of course, every narrator is in control of the reader to some extent – but in the case of the omniscient narrator the reader is aware of the control.)

The 'straight' narrator appears to tell the story without any particular line to any one character's experiences or feelings. This narrative is a kind of reportage.

The third person narrative from one particular character's point of view tells a story through the eyes of the main character (usually) and gives the reader access (limited or free) to that character's feelings and perspectives. Unlike the first person narrative, there can be a feeling of objectivity, despite the reader's connection to one particular person.

The first person narrative is essentially egocentric – the unfolding story is conveyed entirely from the point of view of the character telling it. This will obviously colour the narrative, insofar as the writer wishes the character to do so. This technique is developed further in the monologue (see Chapter 4). At times the use of the first person narrative can make it difficult for the writer to describe the narrator of the story because there is no authorial 'eye'. The character of the first person narrator emerges gradually through the text – it is the physical appearance that is sometimes tricky. There are ways of getting round this. The real cliché is to have the character look in a mirror. Try to avoid anything so obvious! However, clues as to appearance and character can be given in the words of other people, or the narrator can refer to what other people say, combining this with a kind of self-portrait, as in this extract from *Matilda's England* by William Trevor.

> I was going to be pretty, people used to say, although I couldn't see it myself. My hair had a reddish tinge, like my mother's, but it was straight and uninteresting. I had freckles, which I hated, and my eyes were a shade of blue I didn't much care for either. I detested being called Matilda.

A sequence of first person narratives is occasionally found in a longer text than a short story, where the writer can establish differing versions of an experience, and the individual characters' responses to it, by changing the viewpoints. The reader is then placed in a position to make some kind of independent judgment. But this 'independence' is, of course, largely influenced by the writer. A famous example of this approach is found in Wilkie Collins's classic novel of mystery *The Moonstone*.

Read Henry James's long short story *The Turn of the Screw*, in which the writer establishes a complex and subtle shift in narrative viewpoints. This enables James to add to the mystery and ambivalence of the narrative, and places the reader at the heart of the mystery, without being certain of a firm interpretation of the story. Since the narrative turns on good and evil, the ambivalence creates not just narrative uncertainties but also moral ones. Complexity of narrative viewpoint, again creating some ambivalence in the reader's response, is also present in Emily Brontë's novel *Wuthering Heights*.

■ Re-read the extracts **1–10** and try to decide which kind of viewpoint is intended in each case. (Note that extract **9** belongs to the highly stylised genre of the fairy tale, in which narrative viewpoint is traditionally neutral, and in many cases follows a well-known format.)

■ THE DESCRIPTIVE OPENING

Description should never be pasted into a story. It forms part of the texture of writing, and there is infinite variety in the ways it can be created. Sometimes a piece will start with a richly descriptive opening. In some instances it can be very explicit, taking the reader's eye on a visual journey, as if the writer were painting a picture that we 'read'.

Here is the opening of D. H. Lawrence's short story *A Fragment of Stained Glass*, where care has been taken to describe the visual setting.

> Beauvale is, or was, the largest parish in England. It is thinly populated, only just netting the stragglers from shoals of houses in three large mining villages. For the rest, it holds a great tract of woodland, fragment of old Sherwood, a few hills of pasture and arable land, three collieries, and, finally, the ruins of a Cistercian abbey. These ruins lie in a still rich meadow at the foot of the last fall of woodland, through whose oaks shines a blue of hyacinths, like water, in Maytime. Of the abbey, there remains only the east wall of the chancel standing, a wild thick mass of ivy weighting one shoulder, while pigeons perch in the tracery of the lofty window. This is the window in question.

What do you think the author is trying to do here? How do you respond to this opening? See note 2, page 63.

Here is a further example of a rather different technique. Read again the opening two paragraphs of John Steinbeck's short novel *Of Mice and Men*. Now look again at the last section of the novel where the reader is taken once again into the same landscape:

> The deep green pool of the Salinas river was still in the late afternoon. Already the sun had left the valley to go climbing up the slopes of the Gabilan mountains, and the hill-tops were rosy in the sun. But by the pool among the mottled sycamores, a pleasant shade had fallen.

Into this peaceful scene, Lennie emerges and the narrative comes to its inevitable close. The author deliberately revisits and echoes the early description of the setting. Why does he do this? See note 3, page 63.

As well as the detailed, 'painted' visual description there is, also, the description that is deliberately incomplete, working more by well chosen selection – a telling phrase or word. Often the selection is made not only to describe visually but also to give hints, set a mood or give an insight into a character or situation.

■ Look again at extract 5. And look at extract 8 and consider the mood created simply by the selection of the phrase '...the first watery eggs of sweat on his palms...'

■ MAKING A START

When faced with a writing task, particularly in an examination, many writers, whether experienced or inexperienced, feel that they have nothing to say. It can be useful, therefore, to ask yourself a few questions first of all so that you can find access to the raw material you have collected, and a way into the story. You can then concentrate on the opening, aiming to attract the reader's attention, while at the same time focusing on the narrative viewpoint which needs to be established very early on in the story.

■ Here is a suggestion. Let us assume that you have been asked to look at Picture A (page 120) and have been given the task: Think about what it feels like to be left behind or left out. Write the story suggested to you by the face in the picture.

■ With a partner, think about **what** and **where** and **who** and **when**, and make notes for a story.

Where is the child?
Who is the child?
When, at what point in the story, are you going to bring the reader in?
Who is the narrator?

There are many related questions, for example:

Is anyone else there? If so, who – and whereabouts?
What has happened up to this point?
What happens next?
What kind of atmosphere or mood do I want to create?
How will I do this?
What viewpoint will I select – and will this be clearly evident in the opening?

■ From your notes select carefully the clues you want to give the reader early on in the story, and the expectations you want to set up. Remember, you want to awaken the reader's interest and anticipation, to make him or her read on.

■ Now, individually, write the opening paragraph. Re-read it with care, making any changes you want to make. Then discuss with your partner the strengths of each opening paragraph. Working from suggestions and comments, redraft your own paragraph, and go on to write the next one. (Further consultation might persuade you to continue with this piece until you have the first draft of a short story.)

SUMMARY

■ make a good beginning
■ grab the reader's attention
■ when do you want the story to start?
■ where is it happening?
■ who do we meet first?
■ who is telling the story?
■ a descriptive opening can be effective but is not essential

---

■ REFERENCES

1 From the opening of the short story *Anima* by Brian McCabe.
2 From the opening of the short story *Jubilee* by Graham Greene.
3 From the opening of the short story *The Key to My Heart* by V. S. Pritchett.
4 From the opening of the novel *Murther and Walking Spirits* by Robertson Davies.
5 From the opening of the short story *A Sense of Shelter* by John Updike.
6 From the opening of the short story *To Set Our House in Order* by Margaret Laurence.
7 From the opening of the short story *On Saturday Afternoon* by Alan Sillitoe.
8 From the opening of the short story *The Vertical Ladder* by William Sansom.
9 From the opening of the fairy tale *The Magic Fish-Bone* by Charles Dickens.
10 From the opening of the short story *Cross-Country Snow* by Ernest Hemingway.

3

Narrative Writing: description, dialogue, characterisation and ending

■ DESCRIPTIVE WRITING

Generally, you will find that descriptive writing can create the **setting**, the **mood**, and help to build up **characterisation**. Description need not only be visual, it can also be particularly effective when the writer focuses on other senses, and on behavioural idiosyncrasies. In the novel *David Copperfield*, Charles Dickens vividly creates the essence of the character Uriah Heep by conveying, through the narrator David Copperfield, the *physical presence* of the man, particularly as revealed in the narrator's response to him.

> ...I observed that he had not such a thing as a smile about him, and that he could only widen his mouth and make two hard creases down his cheeks, one on each side...

> I observed that his nostrils, which were thin and pointed, with sharp dints in them, had a singular and most uncomfortable way of expanding and contracting themselves...

> ...he frequently ground the palms [of his hands] against each other as if to squeeze them dry and warm, besides often wiping them, in a stealthy way, on his pocket-handkerchief...

> He had a way of writhing when he wanted to express enthusiasm, which was very ugly; and which diverted my attention from the compliment he had paid my relation, to the snaky twistings of his throat and body.

Description can also be slipped into dialogue. For instance:

> 'How haggard you look,' he remarked. 'I hadn't realised just how grey and thin you have grown.'

This kind of descriptive comment allows the reader to see, as it were, without having to be 'told' by the writer to look.

It is therefore important to be tellingly selective in descriptive writing – you want it to engage the readers, rather than swamp them. A significant count of adjectives is more suitable to mathematical calculation than to the craft of writing. Remember that you want to be in control of what and how much you reveal. Description, whether lengthy or merely a word or two, needs to be based on careful and convincing observation. The writer works to create a picture, an effect, an impression, a mood, a character to which the reader responds, sometimes with recognition, sometimes with surprise. But first of all the writer has to have *seen* that picture, *felt* that mood, *known* that person – only then will the description be convincing.

■ Look again at what you have written in response to Picture A (page 120). Have you created the picture, effect, impression, mood that you intended to create? Is there any further hint of description that would help you to achieve this? Work on this – and then consult with your partner about the result.

■ Read D. H. Lawrence's story ***The Blind Man*** (Section Two, page 68) Look again at some of the descriptive passages in the story.

'Give me your arm, dear,' she said.

She pressed his arm close to her, as she went. But she longed to see him, to look at him. She was nervous. He walked erect, with face rather lifted, but with a curious tentative movement of his powerful, muscular legs. She could feel the clever, careful, strong contact of his feet with the earth, as she balanced against him. For a moment he was a tower of darkness to her, as if he rose out of the earth...

Maurice had a curious monolithic way of sitting in a chair, erect and distant. Isabel's heart always beat when she caught sight of him thus...

Maurice was feeling, with curious little movements, almost like a cat kneading her bed, for his place, his knife and his fork, his napkin. He was getting the whole geography of his cover into his consciousness. He sat erect and inscrutable, remote-seeming. Bertie watched the static figure of the blind man, the delicate tactile discernment of the large, ruddy hands, and the curious mindless silence of the brow, above the scar. With difficulty he looked away, and without knowing what he did, picked up a little crystal bowl of violets from the table, and held them to his nose.

The richness and detail of description are an important part of the writer's technique, particularly in these extracts. They vividly connect the reader to Maurice's blindness. How does the writer achieve this? After reading each descriptive piece you should ask yourself: What is really being described? Do you understand more about the story as a whole with each piece of description? See note 4, page 63.

SUMMARY

- description must engage the reader
- it must be convincing, whether drawn from reality or fantasy
- it must, therefore, be based on observation.

■ EFFECTIVE USE OF DIALOGUE

Dialogue not only gives us insight into characters, it can also move a story along. We can learn about events 'outside' the story, off-stage, as it were, by means of what characters say to each other. We can also discover aspects of the **sub-text** through the dialogue. The sub-text is the part of the story that lies beneath the text we actually read; the subtleties, implications, aspects of the story and the characters that the writer allows the reader to infer by hints, faint clues. One of the fascinating aspects of a story, in particular a short story, is what is concealed, hinted at, as well as what is actually revealed. In this respect the short story has strong links with poetry.

When you write dialogue it is important to be true to the sounds and rhythms of spoken language. *Listen* to the speakers in your head. Try to give characters individual voices – voices are individual in real life. If you can achieve this, then your dialogue will form part of your skill in characterisation, giving the reader insights into the characters as well as narrative information. It sometimes helps to think through other aspects of the individuality of a character – a walk, a gesture, a detail like left or right-handedness – that you might not actually write into the story but which helps you to 'build' the character in your imagination. This itself will help you with the dialogue. You might also like to try occasionally writing down overheard snatches of dialogue that you come across, on a bus, in a shop, wherever. Read them attentively: think about the rhythms of the speech, think about the things said and those not said but implied. It would not be surprising to have jotted down something like this, untidy as it might seem from the writer's point of view:

'Look at that! Look at that! Weird. Did you see anything like it? Did you see?'

'Can't find my purse. I mean, it was here a minute ago.'

'Look!'

'Where? Oh yes. Ah, here it is.'

The object of the exercise is not to encourage you to write dialogue from life by necessarily copying the *text* of the dialogue – but by imitating the *rhythms* and the naturalness of dialogue. As a writer creating text you are concerned with *selecting* from life, not recording it. But these selections need to be authentic. Not only should you try to capture the rhythms of speech but also the distinctiveness and genuine sounds of spoken language and dialect.

Let us suppose, for example, that you want the reader to know that someone is in trouble with the law. Instead of *narrating* this, as the all-knowing author, which can become a little tedious if this is the mainstay of your story-telling, you can use dialogue. Something like this:

'Saw the polis car last night, did ye?' Mrs Lindsay, who was standing bulkily in the slow Post Office queue, nudged her next-door neighbour standing beside her. She continued, 'No surprise, ken. Ah mean the kerry-on in that hoose. A' times a day an night. She's a strange wumman, and no mistake.'

As you will appreciate, this not only gives us information which will be essential to the narrative, but also gives us glimpses of a sub-text in its suggestion of mood, and what is revealed to us about Mrs Lindsay.

Consider this dialogue from the first chapter of Iain Crichton Smith's **Consider the Lilies** between an old woman, Mrs Scott, and Patrick Sellar, factor to the Duke of Sutherland.

'What are you looking at?' said her visitor angrily. 'At your land? What good has it ever done you? It's all stone, isn't it? If you had any sense you wouldn't worry about leaving it. This new house will be in the north by the sea.'

But she wasn't looking at the land, she was looking at the churchyard.

'My father and mother are buried in the churchyard,' she said.

'Yes, you people are always talking about the dead.'

Well, why shouldn't they? The dead were always around them. Soon she herself would be dead.

■   Look closely for the subtleties in this extract and think about what the writer conveys by means of them. See note 5, page 64.

■ Work in pairs. Look again at Picture A and your draft so far. Is there any dialogue? If so, might you make changes? If not, would dialogue be appropriate? Discuss with your partner any changes you make, the reasons for them, and your preferences. Re-work the paragraphs you have already written, paying particular attention to any descriptive writing and to dialogue. Discuss with each other what you intend should happen in the story, and map out the next few paragraphs. Now, individually, finish your story. Pay close attention to the descriptive elements, and listen attentively to the dialogue. (If you already have a finished draft, now is the time to re-read it, bearing in mind the processes you have been considering.)

Once again, confer with your partner about what is successful and what needs to be changed. When you are satisfied, read the complete story again. Try to read it not as the *writer* but as a *reader* who has never seen the story before. You should then be able to judge where there is need for alteration. This development of your critical awareness is a very important part of learning to be a writer. When you *tell* a story you will make changes and adaptations according to the responses of the listener(s) to whom you are speaking. When you *write* a story, you have to be both writer *and* reader, and try to think of how the reader will respond to the story. As the writer Julian Barnes suggested, 'There is a lover-like element to the author–reader contact.'

SUMMARY

- good dialogue depends on careful listening
- try to capture authentic sounds and rhythms in your dialogue
- let dialogue move the narrative along
- think about what dialogue conceals as well as reveals
- remember that a story can start with dialogue

■ MOOD AND TONE

These form an integral part of the writer's stance, characterisations and descriptions. Read the opening two sentences of J. D. Salinger's **The Catcher in the Rye**, in which the tone becomes quickly evident – and helps to build up the mood.

You will readily be able to identify specific vocabulary that sets the tone of the novel. But, for the writer, the way to establish tone is not quite as cut and dried as that. It also necessitates entering into a character, viewing experience in a particular way. It is important to know and understand the character, and the circumstances, events and places that give the character shape. To help yourself to do these things as a *writer* you must be able, as a *reader*, to recognise when other writers do them successfully.

Establishing mood can also be done by focusing on a symbol, an object, sound, smell, which can permeate a story and create resonances for the reader to give complexity as well as focus to the narrative. **Odour of Chrysanthemums** by D. H. Lawrence shows how economically and effectively this can be achieved.

- ■ This might be an opportunity to concentrate on the mood you hoped to establish in your writing for Picture A. Have you succeeded? Confer with your partner. Do not be afraid to experiment, even if this involves re-writing – this is part of the craft of writing.

■ CHARACTERISATION

Characterisation is built up in a variety of ways; it develops within the fabric of a narrative. Much will be established by dialogue and by narrative viewpoint. The least successful kind of characterisation is when the writer *tells* the reader, in a didactic way, what a character is like. In reading, as in life, we like to find out for ourselves. There can, however, be suggestions of irony in apparently 'telling' the reader about a character. One well-known example is in the opening paragraph of Jane Austen's novel **Emma**.

> Emma Woodhouse, handsome, clever, and rich, with a comfortable home and happy disposition seemed to unite some of the best blessings of existence; and had lived nearly twenty-one years in the world with very little to distress or vex her.

Because this is at the very beginning of the novel, the use of 'seemed' throws down a challenge to the reader, as does the possible self-centredness of 'very little to distress or vex her'. The implied question is: How will we, the readers, respond to Emma Woodhouse as we get to know her?

The following paragraph, taken from Edith Wharton's short story **Madame de Treymes**, introduces the reader to Mrs Elmer Boykin, an American living with her husband in Paris. The story is narrated in the third person from the point of view of John Durham. What makes this description unusual is that it does not appear to be Durham's view of Mrs Boykin (who, incidentally, is his cousin) but the author's view. In this interjection of the authorial voice, Wharton is able to absolve Durham from being a party to the observations, at the same time forming a bond of confidence with the reader in an item of gossip. Notice how indirect the author is in 'telling' the reader about Mrs Elmer Boykin.

> Mrs. Elmer Boykin was a small plump woman, to whose vague prettiness the lines of middle-age had given no meaning: as though whatever had happened to her had merely added to the sum total of her inexperience. After a Parisian residence of twenty-five years, spent in a state of feverish servitude to the great artists of the Rue de la Paix, her dress and hair still retained a certain rigidity in keeping with the directness of her gaze and the unmodulated candour of her voice. Her very drawing-room had the hard bright atmosphere of her native skies, and one felt that she was still true at heart to the national ideas in electric lighting and plumbing.

In some cases, external attributes (for instance, possessions, setting) can give the reader hints about a character. You will have noticed the importance of external attributes to the characterisation of Mrs Boykin, her rigid hair, the hard brightness of the drawing-room. This indirect portrayal pays off in subtlety. It can be effective to use symbols to build up characters. In a short story such as *Odour of Chrysanthemums*, this can be particularly economic, since symbol can convey to the reader so many resonances of character and narrative, again, rather in the way that imagery in poetry moves the reader, from the shallows of literal comprehension, to finding deeper understanding. Look again at the point in *Odour of Chrysanthemums* when the child, Annie, notices the flower in her mother's apron.

> 'Don't they smell beautiful!'
>
> Her mother gave a short laugh.
>
> 'No,' she said, 'not to me. It was chrysanthemums when I married him, and chrysanthemums when you were born, and the first time they ever brought him home drunk, he'd got brown chrysanthemums in his buttonhole.'

What is the writer doing here? See note 6, page 64.

In a longer text, the focus created by symbol brings the reader back to, and can thus reinforce, the writer's central concerns. An example of this can be found in William Golding's *Lord of the Flies* in which the conch has central and symbolic significance. But let us consider, for a moment, not the conch but Piggy's spectacles which also carry symbolic nuances throughout the novel.

'...Didn't you see what we – what they did?'

There was loathing, and at the same time a kind of feverish excitement in his voice.

'Didn't you see, Piggy?'

'Not all that well. I only got one eye now. You ought to know that, Ralph.'
(Chapter 10)

And, later:

...Piggy paused for a moment and peered round at the dim figures. The shape of the old assembly, trodden in the grass, listened to him.

'I'm going to him with this conch in my hands. I'm going to hold it out. Look, I'm goin' to say, you're stronger than I am and you haven't got asthma. You can see, I'm goin' to say, and with both eyes. But I don't ask for my glasses back, not as a favour. I don't ask you to be a sport, I'll say, not because you're strong, but because what's right's right. Give me my glasses, I'm goin' to say – you got to!'
(Chapter 11)

Sometimes, as in extract 9 (page 11), the genre creates its own 'rules' of characterisation, and the reader's expectations are met by the lightest of hints.

There was once a King, and he had a Queen, and he was the manliest of his sex, and she was the loveliest of hers.

The expectation set up in the reader by 'King' and 'Queen' combined with 'manliest' and 'loveliest' is that these are 'good' characters. And that will probably suffice throughout the tale, because this is a fairy tale and belongs to a genre that creates narrative in a particular and predictable way. In a sense, these characters are themselves symbols. Characters are 'good' and 'bad' and the reader learns to make the distinction very early on, and usually that is all the reader wants to know about a character. Characters rarely develop. Prince Charming is just that, charming, from start to finish. The focus of the fairy tale is the interaction between good and evil, rather than the development or interaction of character in relation to other people and in response to experience.

In the narrative fiction pieces that you will write it is important not only to present characters in an interesting way but also to allow them to develop in the presentation as well as in the narrative. A useful technique in presenting a character can be to use other characters to do it for you. This is normally done by means of dialogue. It is a technique with parallels in real life in that, if you listen to two or three people discussing someone you do not know, you will inevitably build up some kind of picture of that person. For a writer, the subtlety lies in the extent to which the 'gossips' can be trusted. To what extent do they filter or distort the impressions?

■ Read Ernest Hemingway's *A Clean, Well-Lighted Place* (Section Two, page 81). Consider what you come to understand about the old man and the two waiters, and on what your understanding is based. See note 7, page 64.

■ Try an exercise in building up character by imagining the messages that are left on a telephone answering machine over a period of a few days. Thinking about how other characters in a story relate to the main character(s) will help give depth to your own understanding of the character(s).

Generally characters are created by the very process of the writer allowing the reader to get to know them. In the opening pages of *Lord of the Flies* 'the boy with fair hair' and 'the fat boy' suggest, in the childlike quality of these descriptions, a tale of simplicity and innocence. This is echoed in the descriptions of the island paradise:

> Within the irregular arc of coral the lagoon was still as a mountain lake – blue of all shades and shadowy green and purple.

> He undid the snake-clasp of his belt, lugged off his shorts and pants, and stood there naked, looking at the dazzling beach and the water.

But as we read further the complexity of human existence is built up layer by layer: 'the boy with fair hair' becomes Ralph and 'the fat boy' becomes Piggy. Golding gradually reveals the reason for the boys' presence on the island. More characters are introduced, and, as we begin to understand that the boys have histories, so we also witness and become involved in the boys' attempts to control their present – and their fears. Inexorably Golding takes the reader from the innocence of the opening through the experience of the narrative – until finally the boys and the island are changed utterly:

> His voice rose under the black smoke before the burning wreckage of the island...with filthy body, matted hair, and unwiped nose, Ralph wept for the end of innocence, the darkness of man's heart, and the fall through the air of the true, wise friend called Piggy.

SUMMARY

- characterisation is best developed throughout the narrative
- it emerges through dialogue and narrative viewpoint
- it can be revealed symbolically by connections to inanimate things
- character can be tellingly revealed through other characters

---

■ THE ENDING

Solomon Grundy,
Born on Monday,
Christened on Tuesday,
Married on Wednesday,
Took ill on Thursday,
Worse on Friday,
Died on Saturday,
Buried on Sunday.
This is the end
Of Solomon Grundy.

Most learner writers find endings difficult. This is not at all surprising. Having tried to establish some kind of shape to the chaos of ideas, the writer is faced with that final, neat point of resolution – as if the neatness and finality could be readily determined. But, of course, they cannot. Except in the case of Solomon Grundy, life itself is by nature untidy. Nevertheless, the writer is compelled to 'tidy things up' somehow. The best advice is to recognise that in some way you will find the end in the beginning. In George Mackay Brown's *The Bright Spade*, the winter season is over. Jacob puts his spade away in the shed, hoping, as he speaks to it,

> 'that I won't be needing you again till after the shearing and the lobster fishing and the harvest.'

In *Lord of the Flies* the end of the novel is in painful contrast to the beginning. In *Of Mice and Men* there is a deliberate, ironic link between the beginning and the end. It might be helpful to refer here to E. M. Forster's definition of plot, taken from his series of lectures collected in *Aspects of the Novel* (1927):

> 'The king died and then the queen died,' is a story. 'The king died and then the

queen died of grief' is a plot... Consider the death of the queen. If it is in a story we say 'and then?' If it is in a plot we ask 'why?'

In a sense, it is your responsibility to make sure that by the end of your story you have helped the reader to understand 'why'. And, for the writer, that 'why?' is the very essence of the narrative and must be pondered from the beginning.

Sometimes, you might find an idea for the beginning and the end – but you have no ideas for the story itself. Rather like William Boyd's character Charlie, in *Not Yet, Jayette* (Section Two, page 85):

It's a great final scene. Only problem is I'm having some difficulty writing my way towards it. Still, it'll come, I guess.

Charlie's problem is that he hasn't begun to consider the 'why?' of the piece (it's a play) but he has a strong visual picture of the end. He hasn't worked out what might be called the psychology of the action.

As soon as you start to have ideas for a story and characters to give these shape, then you have the ending – which is really only the completion of the shape, an understanding of how people will act and interact. If you find that you have thought of a beginning but have no idea for an ending, take a few moments, at this early stage, to jot down two or three possibilities for the resolution of your ideas. Do not simply wander into the story without having thought about the terrain. How you actually create the ending is then up to you. You will have to guard against being too abrupt, too obvious, too far-fetched, too insipid. But you must be prepared to experiment, to try different endings, just as you have tried different viewpoints for Picture A.

- ■ By this time you will have finished your first draft in response to Picture A. Read it right through. Are you satisfied that you have given it the kind of shape you want? You should be clear that you have established the **setting**, the **narrative viewpoint** and the **mood**. Look critically at the **ending**. This should feel appropriate to all that has gone before. After all, you have taken a lot of trouble to craft the story to this point. Again, discuss it with a partner. You will learn a lot from such discussion.

- ■ Read again the story *The Blind Man*. With a partner, discuss your reactions to each of the three characters and how your views change through the story. For each character, identify what happens, or what is said or narrated, to bring about even the slightest change in your views about the character. Jot down your findings and the page references. Now compare your response to Maurice at the beginning of the story with what you feel at the end. Can you identify what the writer has done throughout the story to bring about the responses you have and the changes that might have occurred? Do you consider the end to be successful? What kind of ending would you have preferred? Try writing your own.

You should now have the confidence to experiment with the short story on your own. You might find it helpful to use one of the other pictures in Section Two as a starting point. But by now you should be able to find your ideas in what you see and hear around you, and let these connect with – and fire – your imagination.

SUMMARY

- the ending is often signposted in the beginning
- the ending completes the reader's understanding of the story – e.g. motive, characterisation
- the ending must be appropriate to the shape of the whole piece, not just tacked on

4

Monologue and Drama

Monologue is a form of narrative that shares characteristics with drama in that people, experiences, ideas and events are presented to the reader through the voice of a particular character – in the case of monologue, only one character – often at a time of tension, conflict or crisis.

There are essentially two forms of monologue:

interior monologue
exterior or dramatic monologue.

Interior monologue is the voice within the head to which the reader is given access. The speaker has no other listener. **Dramatic monologue** is directed to a listener (and to the reader, obviously). This means that in some way the listener is likely to be sufficiently interested in, and involved with, the speaker to be receptive. It is, of course, possible to indicate, in the monologue, the speaker's awareness of the listener. Such awareness enters into the text of the monologue itself. Something like...

You look shocked. Believe me every word is true...

As audiences, we are perhaps more familiar with this kind of monologue in the dramatic form on television or on stage, where we can see the character *and* see the character's responses to the listener(s) without these having somehow to be implied in the text. An example of staged dramatic monologue where we, the audience, are in fact the listeners is Rikki Fulton's *Late Call* with the Rev. I. M. Jolly. Another example of monologue is the dramatic soliloquy. As you will know from reading Shakespeare, there is a distinction to be made between the soliloquy in which the character speaks his thoughts (interior monologue) and that in which the character speaks directly to the audience (sometimes to share a plot, a secret – which is more of an aside).

You will also be familiar with dramatic monologue in poetry. A notable

31

example is Robert Browning's *My Last Duchess*, in which Browning creates the strong presence of the listener as well as the tellingly revealing portrait of the speaker. In more recently written work, you will find that the late Dorothy Parker, American writer and wit, has a number of well-crafted prose monologues; and Anne Fine's novel *The Killjoy* is in its entirety a sustained dramatic monologue.

Experimenting with the writing of monologue can be fun – and trains the ear to hear a voice, and to establish tone. These all help you with dramatic sequences and to develop characterisation. In this genre of writing, the starting point must always be the character. And you need to know that character very well indeed. Inch by inch you will reveal to the reader only what you intend to reveal, building up the narrative and the characterisation by this means. Initially, there will be a context – reason and circumstances – for the monologue, and, in the case of dramatic monologue, there will be a listener.

As when writing dialogue in narrative (see Chapter 3) you need to capture an authentic voice for the speaker. So you need to listen carefully to the rhythms of speech and thought that you are trying to establish. The important thing to remember is that the monologue must be in the spoken (or inner) voice of the character, although other people might be quoted, and there might be cause for change of tone, mood, even dialect, within the monologue. Overall, the piece needs to portray the character of the speaker as well as tell a 'story'. The reader should be left with a strong sense of a character created (again, as in drama).

■ Read *You Should Have Seen the Mess* by Muriel Spark (Section Two, page 89). What does the writer do to create your response to the speaker? See note 8, page 64.

When you attempt to write interior monologue you might find it easier to be personal, to make the voice your own – or at least to start off this way. It should not be too challenging to think of an episode – perhaps where there was conflict – in which you gave vent to your feelings and thoughts in a monologue stream within your head. Try to capture such an episode in writing. You will find on occasion that it can be effective to counterpoint interior monologue with exterior monologue. Imagine, for instance, that the central character finds himself or herself having to deal with a difficult customer: you could counterpoint the interior monologue flow with a few politely spoken remarks. One of the attractive aspects of writing interior monologue is the chance simply to let thoughts flow. In fact, although this is a

characteristic of the genre, it must nevertheless always be controlled by you –
something that can be refined by redrafting.

■ MAKING A START

■ Look at Picture **B** (page 121). Allow your imagination to work on the
starkness of the scene. Write an internal monologue for the person in the
picture. Think very carefully about the opening words; they might, for
instance, start in the middle of a train of thought. These opening words
will give you the direction of the monologue. Choose another picture
(or idea of your own) where there is a possibility of speaker and listener,
and write a dramatic monologue. Again, think very carefully about the
opening words.

■ Working in pairs, read the monologues aloud to each other. You will
readily hear if the voice you have created is authentic.

SUMMARY

■ the events (the narrative) of the monologue must emerge clearly
■ the speaker's voice must be authentic
■ the character of the speaker needs to be convincingly brought to life
■ in dramatic monologue the relationship between speaker and listener
needs to be established for the reader

■ Read *Not Yet, Jayette* by William Boyd (Section Two, page 85).
Compare, with a partner, your responses to Charlie. Try to identify how
Boyd has made you respond as you do. See note 9, page 64.

■ WRITING DRAMATIC SCENES

From writing stories and monologues it is a short step to writing dramatic
episodes.
   Read *Request Stop* by Harold Pinter (Section Two, page 93). This short
revue sketch demonstrates the dramatic possibilities of monologue. If you
look at the points in the summary above you will appreciate how economic

and effective the piece is – as well as humorous. Note also the mileage Pinter gets from his use of pauses. It is worth remembering at this point that much of the narrative of life is *not* spoken. It is a natural temptation for the apprentice writer to think that drama is created only with words. This is not necessarily so. The challenge remains: how to 'write' the silences so that the reader senses when things are left out, hidden, stumbled over. A further point is that the writer needs to know (and to convey in stage directions) just what the characters on stage are doing when they are not actually speaking.

Another misconception often held by the inexperienced writer is that the dialogue of drama (or indeed of narrative) is linear and somehow moves only forwards. Again, this is not necessarily so; it frequently has a kind of overlapping, non-sequential quality. Take some time to listen to a group of people talking, and notice the repetitions, the things misheard, the lack of attention – at times the disconnection between people who are supposedly talking to each other. Look at *Last to Go*, the other revue sketch by Pinter (Section Two, page 95). You will find examples of this 'overlapping' and disconnection. Try acting it out with a partner.

In drama, the audience's understanding of what happens (the narrative) is created entirely by the dialogue and the action, and to some extent, the location. How the actors speak their lines, how they move and what they do on stage is indicated to them (and to the director) by the stage directions. So stage directions are a critical part of the written text.

When writing drama you do not rely mainly on *telling* the reader, as in the story; you also *show* the audience. And character is revealed as much by how a person behaves as by what he or she says. This is rather different from narrative writing where the narrative itself, rather than the dialogue, has to reveal behaviour. For instance, in a story you might find:

'Don't ever speak to me like that again.' She spoke quietly but with menace.

In drama, the quiet tone and the menace would be conveyed by tone of voice and body language – and, of course, by the positional relationship between the characters, where and how they stand or turn away, or whatever. These subtleties will have to be written into the stage directions so that a director can bring the printed text to life on the stage. Stage directions, therefore, are the critical link between the writer's intentions and the director's realisation of these for the audience. Some dramatists write very clear and detailed directions. As you will notice when reading *Pygmalion*, George Bernard Shaw is one such dramatist. Consider, for instance, the episode at the end of Act I:

The flower girl [*rising in desperation*] You ought to be stuffed with nails, you ought. [*Flinging the basket at his feet*] Take the whole blooming basket for sixpence.

[*The church clock strikes the second quarter.*]

Higgins [*hearing in it the voice of God, rebuking him for his Pharisaic want of charity to the poor girl*] A reminder. [*He raises his hat solemnly; then throws a handful of money into the basket and follows Pickering.*]

The flower girl [*picking up a half-crown*] Ah-ow-ooh! [*Picking up a couple of florins*] Aaah-ow-ooh! [*Picking up several coins*] Aaaaaah-ow-ooh! [*Picking up a half-sovereign*] Aaaaaaaaaaaah-ow-ooh!!!

[*The church clock strikes the second quarter.*]

Not only does Shaw supply detailed stage directions but also, at the beginning of every act – or when introducing a character to the action – he supplies the director and actor with detailed descriptions. Look at the point, in Act II, when we first meet Alfred Doolittle:

Alfred Doolittle is an elderly but vigorous dustman, clad in the costume of his profession, including a hat with a back brim covering his neck and shoulders. He has well marked and rather interesting features, and seems equally free from fear and conscience. He has a remarkably expressive voice, the result of a habit of giving vent to his feelings without reserve. His present pose is that of wounded honour and stern resolution.

You will notice that Shaw's description goes deeper than appearance.

If you choose to write dramatic texts you are likely to be creating quite short, self-contained pieces, single scenes (probably opening scenes), or perhaps an episode for a serial. Your concern, therefore, will be to set the scene, introduce characters and establish conflict (or some kind of tension, which could also be comic) as swiftly and as economically as possible. A lot depends on the characters in a drama being three-dimensional, particularly the central characters who hold the action and the narrative together. Try to create characters with muscle, rather than flab. They will give you (and the audience) better mileage.

With a partner, view a few of the *Fawlty Towers* episodes – especially the one featuring the hotel guest who dies. Study this particular episode and make a note of the storylines within it that you consider important, the characters (apart from the hotel staff) who feature prominently and the 'clues' that the audience is given so that the whole piece ties together at the end. This is best done by viewing it right through first then re-viewing it to appreciate the technique and the economy. Discuss with your partner how you think the humour is achieved. Note the clues that are given the viewer as to the direction the narrative takes. See note 10, page 64.

■ MAKING A START

As with any other kind of writing you need to start with an idea. In the case of drama you need a central idea which has 'explosive' possibilities.

■ Look at Picture **C** (page 122). Let us assume that you have been asked to write, in no more than 1500 words, the opening scene of a play that is suggested to you by this picture, with the young woman as the central character.

You see a crowded pub where a woman is sitting alone with a travel bag. You know that she is the central character. Who will be the other characters? What has happened to bring her to this point? Is she running – or waiting? What is prominent in her background: friends, family, husband, job? Success, failure? (You will have your own questions to ask.) Where will the drama take place – what will be the main scene? Where will the piece start – long before this scene in the photograph, or just before it? Perhaps even with this scene. How much information do you need to give the director about the main characters and the location? Once you have decided on your opening scene and location, decide who is present. What stage directions might you need right at the beginning and throughout? Who speaks first? (And why?) You might find it helpful to use a storyboard layout at first. Eight to ten frames will probably give you enough of a focus. Write the first draft of your drama piece from this.

■ Check that your textual layout and stage directions conform to the conventions of drama writing. Now try out this draft with a partner (or small group, if this is possible). This will allow you to hear whether the dialogue is authentic or wooden. It will also alert you to the effectiveness of your stage directions. Later on you might wish to return to this piece of writing to work over and complete it for your collection of writing.

Here are a few more ideas that might help to keep you writing in this genre:

a secret revealed
the main character misses a train (or plane or bus)
bad news (by phone, letter, message, mistake)
someone returns home to find an unwelcome visitor
someone meets his/her double

It goes without saying that the preliminary contextualisation that you need to apply to the writing of narrative (see Chapters 2 and 3) will also apply here. You should, for instance, have a very clear picture and knowledge of the characters and of how they will interact with each other. You should be able to convey how they will speak and move (establishing the sub-text). You should also have decided what has happened before the scene/play opens, and you should be able to anticipate the end, not in detail, perhaps, but in essence.

■ For further practice choose one of the ideas above (or one of your own). Identify the main characters. Decide on the principle location and the possible changes of scene. Select a particular point at which the action will start. Who will speak first? Next? What stage directions are needed? Now let the dialogue start the action, and then complete the opening scene. Use a storyboard, if you find it helpful. When you feel that it is gathering momentum, start to review what you have written, paying particular attention to the authenticity of the dialogue.

SUMMARY

- ■ dramatic writing needs a location
- ■ it needs characters
- ■ it needs authentic dialogue
- ■ it needs stage directions
- ■ the context for the drama is created through dialogue and action (bringing stage directions to life)

■ WRITING FOR RADIO

If you choose to write drama for radio you will need to have a clear understanding of how the needs of a radio audience differ from those of a viewing audience. Although the scene is not presented visually, it must present to the audience sufficient aural information for the inner eye to imagine the scene. This means that dialogue and judicious use of sound effects are critically important in giving the listeners access to what is happening, who is involved, and where it is happening.

The obvious temptation for the apprentice writer is to use dialogue to 'explain' the narrative. Avoid this, since it is not the way we actually talk, and would make tedious listening. Developing techniques for setting the scene is therefore very important. It might be useful to ask yourself exactly what needs to be heard by the audience to help their understanding. And, for the director, stage directions are crucially important since they must also cover sound effects. Look again at Picture **C**. If you decide that your opening scene will take place within the pub then you could easily establish the location with typical sounds of a pub, and snatches of dialogue. (For instance, *Two pints of heavy, mate...* or something to that effect.) But remember that the sounds you want to let the listeners hear have first to be written as stage directions for the director. And if the sounds involve dialogue, you would need to establish that this is 'background' dialogue – as in the example above.

In radio drama, the introduction of the characters to the audience must also be handled carefully. The listeners will need to know who the speakers are, where they are, how many there are, and be given some indication of the physical relationship (as well as other kinds of relationship) between the characters. For instance:

> Mind if I join you?
> I told you to leave me alone.

gives the listener quite a lot to go on and gives you scope for development of the dramatic narrative.

> Mind if I join you?
> I told you to leave me alone, Ian.
> Janet, listen. Janet!...

gives the listener more to go on because names are given. But indicating the names so early on could sound false, so this might have to be delayed. What is important is that you think about this kind of detail and always listen for the authenticity in the dialogue.

■ Try writing for radio the first scene of the stage piece you have already drafted.

SUMMARY

- radio drama makes additional demands on the writer because it is for a listening audience
- sound effects are very important in establishing scene and location
- dialogue needs to give the listener as much information as possible without *explaining*

In writing dramatic episodes – whether for viewing or for listening audiences – you also need to consider the production of the piece, and be realistic about it. There is no special effects team ready to translate your far-fetched or over-ambitious ideas into something workable, so you have to make sure that your text is realisable. A common weakness with inexperienced dramatists is to have far too many changes of scene: in a street, in a pub, in the swimming baths, up a hill. Since you will be writing short dramatic pieces, try to keep your locations tight. And, as you well know, some of the most dramatic episodes can take place in a shoe-box-sized location – all you really need are people.

■ Look again at Picture **C** and the radio and stage versions of the scene that you have written. Observe the essential differences that you have made. Which do you think is more successful?

5

Poetry

Poetry can offer the reader a close, intimate and private relationship with a subject. How a poem comes to life is an individual experience for each reader. This is probably because poetry is concise and elliptical, and each reader 'rounds out' the ellipse, the flattened circle, in a personal way. The connections that the reader makes between reality and the imagination are inspired by the language of the poetry. Poetry is also characterised by imagery, and each reader creates from the images his or her own picture. Read the following poem by Thomas Hardy. As you read you will be searching for meaning but also for understanding of what lies beneath the surface meaning. What helps you to do this, to round out the ellipse?

I Look into My Glass

I look into my glass,
And view my wasting skin,
And say, 'Would God it came to pass
My heart had shrunk as thin!'

For then I, undistrest
By hearts grown cold to me,
Could lonely wait my endless rest
With equanimity.

But Time, to make me grieve,
Part steals, lets part abide;
And shakes this fragile frame at eve
With throbbings of noontide.

See note 11, page 65.

The conciseness of poetry, linked to the possibilities of interpretation that it offers the reader, presents the writer with a distinct challenge: to create, within a carefully determined form, something that can take the reader into a closer understanding of the topic (and often of the self). In responding to this challenge the writer needs to consider carefully the weight of every word used – for appropriateness of rhythm, resonance, symbol and sensory impact, as well as for obvious meaning. Think, for example, about Hardy's use of *thin* in the first stanza, and think of the association of ideas this sets up in you.

I Look into My Glass is a very introspective poem, and compels the reader to look inwards. Let us consider a poem that has a public, rather than a private, focus. But here, too, the selection of images and ideas works movingly. Here is the end of Edwin Muir's poem in blank verse **The Good Town**, which brings before the reader recognition of aspects of the world in which we live. Although written soon after the Second World War, it could have been written yesterday, for the truth it still shows.

> '...No: when evil comes
> All things turn adverse, and we must begin
> At the beginning, heave the groaning world
> Back in its place again, and clamp it there.
> Then all is hard and hazardous. We have seen
> Good men made evil wrangling with the evil,
> Straight minds grown crooked fighting crooked minds.
> Our peace betrayed us; we betrayed our peace.
> Look at it well. This was the good town once.'
>
> These thoughts we have, walking among our ruins.

There is no topic, thought, idea, emotion that cannot be treated in poetry. Pause for a moment, and allow yourself to dwell on something – a thought, an object, a person, an animal, an idea, a memory, something glimpsed through the window. Start with this and write six short lines to convey to a partner what it is you are thinking about. Did you succeed?

In trying to bring your subject alive for the reader you will perhaps be tempted to describe it, to write *about* it. The advice of many poets would be: Don't! Instead, try to bring your subject to life in a different way: through the senses, making the connections by imagery, or (as in the extract from Edwin Muir's poem) by understatement. '*This was the good town once*' and '*walking among ruins*' are pregnant with all that is not said. In his book **Poetry in the Making**, Ted Hughes advises:

> ...imagine what you are writing about. See it and live it. Do not think it up laboriously, as if you were working out mental arithmetic. Just look at it, touch it, smell it, listen to it, turn yourself into it. When you do this, the words look

after themselves... You keep your eyes, your ears, your nose, your taste, your touch, your whole being on the thing you are turning into words.

Hughes himself provides a clear example of the approach he advocates in his poem *The Jaguar*.

Let us take another example. Focus on a time when you were very angry. The discipline you impose on yourself is the concentration on the moment, the focus. You have to decide how much needs to be explained before the moment of incandescence; how best to convey the experience of anger through the senses, through imagery, by what is not stated, rather than by *telling* the reader about it. Let the reader *feel* it, *imagine* it, *guess* it, as you feel it, imagine it, and imply it. This could amount to the difference between writing something like:

I felt very angry

and

My eyes burned, hot and red

and

My burning eyes

Jot down the words and phrases that help you to re-experience the *sense* of anger. Now decide upon the shape you want to make with these words. Is there some narrative? Are you focusing upon the heat of the moment, or later, in reflection? Work from your jottings. You will probably need several drafts – don't try to achieve the final piece all at once. Let your ideas simmer. Revisit the text, and refine it each time. All writing repays this treatment, but particularly poetry.

Read *Telephone Conversation* by Wole Soyinka. How successfully is the emotion portrayed? See note 12, page 65.

Then read Liz Lochhead's poem *Revelation* and notice particularly the sensory impact of the following lines, which bring the bull to life and pull the reader into the very centre of the child's experience:

At first, only black
and the hot reek of him. Then he was immense,
his edges merging with the darkness, just
a big bulk and a roar to be really scared of,

a trampling, and a clanking tense with the chain's jerk.
His eyes swivelled in the great wedge of his tossed head.
He roared his rage. His nostrils gaped...

I ran, my pigtails thumping on my back in fear...
only my small and shaking hand on the jug's rim
in case the milk should spill.

■ MAKING A START

■ Select one of the Pictures **B**, **D** or **G** (pages 121, 123 and 126). Discuss with a partner the focus, or emphasis, you wish to make. For instance, in the case of Picture B you might want to establish the essential loneliness of the woman. What would be your focus? This will give you your structure. The emptiness of the scene? The woman's expression, or solitariness? In choosing Picture **G** you might decide to use the symbol of the implicit contrast (for instance, in the disturbing juxtaposition of bed and street). Concentrate on the essential impact of the picture. In Picture **D** you might consider that the heart of the picture lies in the child's expression.

■ When you have found your focus, 'let the words look after themselves', as Ted Hughes suggests. Write down those words and phrases that *capture*, rather than *describe*, the essence of what you feel and want to say. Share and discuss your jottings with a partner, then, individually, clarify the focus and discard everything that does not contribute to this.

In writing – particularly in writing poetry – you must be prepared to discard a lot as you go over it and pare it down. Again, discuss with your partner at this stage before making further drafts. These discussions should help in your own critical development – essential, when you are called upon to write on your own.

SUMMARY

■ poetry is notably concise and often elliptical
■ it is characterised by use of imagery
■ it can often be characterised by understatement or indirect statement
■ each reader will find an individual way into the poem
■ focusing on the senses rather than on description makes more immediate impact
■ writing poetry requires a lot of re-reading and refining

■ SIMILE

You might find it helpful to spend a little time concentrating on simile. For most poets this is an essential tool of the trade. Forget your school book exercises on 'the simile'. The point of using simile is to make connections, to clarify and to make deeper the connections between reality and the imagination, and to let these connections work in the reader's imagination. Here are a few of the many examples to be found in *The Eve of St Agnes* by John Keats:

> Sudden a thought came like a full-blown rose,
> Flushing his brow, and in his pained heart
> Made purple riot ...

> But to her heart, her heart was voluble,
> Paining with eloquence her balmy side;
> As though a tongueless nightingale should swell
> Her throat in vain, and die, heart-stifled, in her dell.

> Into her dream he melted, as the rose
> Blendeth its odour with the violet, –
> Solution sweet: meantime the frost-wind blows
> Like Love's alarum pattering the sharp sleet
> Against the window-panes;

When we wish to deepen the impact of a description – to move from the surface factual ordinariness to the imaginative possibilities – we search for comparisons to convey resonances of association and meaning. You can hear young children doing this all the time in their story-telling, reaching into their imaginations to find a comparison to make the impact that 'mere' reality does not seem to offer. So we might say:

> She had pale skin

or

> She had skin like alabaster.

They do not mean the same thing, of course. And it's no use putting fancy work like *alabaster* into your writing if it gives the wrong message or evokes the wrong kind of associations. Nevertheless, an exercise such as this, which focuses attention on making connections, can build confidence and be fun to do.

■ Work with a partner, comparing similes, taking it in turns to make a statement and supply the simile. Remember, you are not only looking for similes for concrete things but also for abstract ones. (It is worth mentioning here that connections can very effectively be implied by highlighting difference and contrast, as well as similarity.) Here are some suggestions to get you started:

church bells
selfishness
the smell of baking
a lochside at dusk
loneliness
an overcast sky

In addition read Brian McCabe's poem *Comparisons* (Section Two, page 97) which explores – with both lightness and seriousness – the contrast between finding similes to make connections, and a literal response to experience.

■ METAPHOR

Metaphor takes the reader beyond the direct comparison suggested by simile. In the metaphor comparison becomes the statement itself, and reality is made even more immediate through the imaginative power of the image. Look at this poem, *Arms and the Boy*, by Wilfred Owen:

Let the boy try along this bayonet-blade
How cold steel is, and keen with hunger of blood;
Blue with all malice, like a madman's flash;
And thinly drawn with famishing for flesh.

Lend him to stroke these blind, blunt bullet-heads
Which long to nuzzle in the hearts of lads,
Or give him cartridges of fine zinc teeth,
Sharp with the sharpness of grief and death.

For his teeth seem for laughing round an apple,
There lurk no claws behind his fingers supple;
And God will grow not talons at his heels,
Nor antlers through the thickness of his curls.

Which images make the greatest impact on you? Can you explain how the poet has achieved this? See note 13, page 65.

Metaphor is the very life of poetry. Have a look at Norman MacCaig's short poem *Boundaries*, which has a beautifully simple and sustained image. And look at this first stanza from G.M. Hopkins's poem *Inversnaid*:

> This darksome burn, horseback brown,
> His rollrock highroad rolling down,
> In coop and in comb the fleece of his foam
> Flutes and low to the lake falls home.

And the powerful opening of Dylan Thomas's *Do Not Go Gentle into that Good Night*:

> Do not go gentle into that good night,
> Old age should burn and rave at close of day;
> Rage, rage against the dying of the light.

As you will find, when you read the complete poems, it is not only metaphor that powerfully illuminates description and meaning in all these examples, but also rhythm.

SUMMARY

- simile makes the connection between reality and the imagination
- it is an essential tool for the poet
- metaphor transforms reality through imagination into something memorable and individual to each reader
- metaphor gives the poem artistry – and sometimes its immortality

---

■ RHYTHM AND RHYME

All poems have rhythm – all language has rhythm – but not all poems have rhyme. When we write it isn't only ideas and thoughts that take shape but also the individual sounds and beat of the words and phrases in which each person expresses thought: our verbalising of thought forms sound-patterns that help to make understanding more immediate.

The bold, beautiful baroness

reaches our understanding speedily and sets up different expectations from

the baroness was a fine-looking woman and had a lot of courage!

All specific poetic forms have distinctive patterns, each has a particular rhythm (metre) and rhyming scheme. Your reading of sonnets, for example, will have taught you this. Free verse is without apparent constraints. But it is challenging to write well, because the writer in fact needs to create his or her own form, and find the rhythms that allow it to *become* verse, and not collected words and phrases lined up to resemble verse. Listen for the artistry in the poetry you read, and read aloud your own poetic writing, training yourself to listen for the effectiveness of the rhythm and, where appropriate, the resolution of sound that rhyme brings.

Rhyme gives poetry a very musical quality. And, as in music, it seems to give lines (and sometimes half lines) a cadence that brings the piece back to its musical key. It also offers the writer the challenge of working within a clear and tight structure. Here is Robert Frost's poem *Stopping by Woods on a Snowy Evening*.

Whose woods these are I think I know.
His house is in the village though;
He will not see me stopping here
To watch his woods fill up with snow.

My little horse must think it queer
To stop without a farmhouse near
Between the woods and frozen lake
The darkest evening of the year.

He gives his harness bells a shake
To ask if there is some mistake.
The only other sound's the sweep
Of easy wind and downy flake.

The woods are lovely, dark and deep,
But I have promises to keep,
And miles to go before I sleep,
And miles to go before I sleep.

To the reader, the poem conveys the utmost simplicity. But consider the writer's skill and artistry in achieving such simplicity. Look at the structure of the rhyming pattern that is woven into the whole poem. Frost works within this structure to produce a poem of eloquence and simplicity.

SUMMARY

- rhythm in poetry guides the reader towards understanding
- rhyme contributes music and cadence to a poem and gives emphasis to understanding
- always read your work aloud so that you can hear if the rhythm (and rhyme) help your poem to sound (and mean) as you would wish

Poetry encompasses such a wide variety of forms it would not be possible to try to write in all of them. Whatever the form, ballad, sonnet, lyric, concrete poetry, or any other, the poem offers the reader a pathway into understanding and interpreting experience that is generally rather different from that offered by other literary forms. This is perhaps particularly so because it finds focus in its containment. Try to find a form which you feel suits you, and experiment with a number of different topics. Many people like to work in a form of free verse, but you might also wish to try out the added discipline of regular metre and rhyme, and perhaps limit the number of stanzas. The more limits you impose on yourself, the greater the challenge – but also the more likely you are to discipline yourself to reach the nub of your idea, and to find your poetic voice because your focus is sharpened.

There is no short-cut to gaining experience in writing poetry. Reading a wide variety of poetry will give you the confidence to experiment in writing it and help you to write honestly and with your own voice. Too often a collection of obscure thoughts arranged under a title is submitted as a poem. Resist the temptation to do this.

Here are some suggestions to get you started:

> a moment in childhood
> the morning after
> a place where you belong
> a series of poems about people – these could include the politician,
>   an old man, the beauty queen, the boy/girl next door
> the sea at night.
> geese on the wing

- When you have tried these suggestions, look at Picture **F** (page 125) and write a poem in response to it. Remember, the first step is to find your way into the topic, your focus. The next is to determine the form you want to use; then set your senses and intellect free to make your connections between the real and the imagined. Write down the words that form these connections. After that, you must read your work over critically and concentrate on the appropriateness and detail of rhyme, rhythm and imagery. You will find that you will make numerous changes, particularly if you leave some time between each reading. That is as it should be. Poems are brief – and every sound and syllable counts.

6

Personal Writing and Reflective Writing

You possibly had early experience of personal writing in the daily diary that you wrote in primary school. The results of this exercise are often repetitive, even formulaic, and reveal little of the individuality of the writer. Day after day half the class is likely to write

> Went home after school. Had my tea. Played football with my pals. Watched TV. Went to bed.

The essential characteristic of the genre is that it should be *personal* – a strong sense of the individual person should be conveyed to the reader. You do not actually have to write about yourself: you might wish to create a persona through whom you write the piece. Remember, you are the writer. It is up to you to decide what you want to write and how best to do it.

Writing of a personal kind is most likely to be found in:

> a diary
> letters
> autobiography
> a will
> a collection of memos

An example of this kind of writing with which you are likely to be familiar is *The Diary of Anne Frank*. The difference between this and any such writing that you might do for certificate purposes is that this was a genuine diary, written as the days passed, not a piece deliberately created and crafted (although creativity and craftsmanship are clearly present). It is not essentially imagined – or invented – such as yours would be in response to a task set, a deadline or an examination.

In selecting any of these formats for personal writing you will still essentially be concerned with shaping a narrative (see Chapter 2). You must still select, prune and shape the piece so that the reader can share in the story or follow the thoughts of the persona. Autobiography and diary entries have a form that is closest to narrative. A collection of one person's letters can form an interesting and autobiographical way of telling a story, describing events, conveying character and reflecting on any of these. Such a collection could be 'found' after a person's death so that the letters cast a personal light on the life that might not have been known before. A touching example of this approach can be found in Bernard MacLaverty's short story *Secrets* (Section Two, page 98).

Whatever kind of writing you are attempting it is as well to remember the powerful force of personal detail and revelation that can be contained in letters (or any other form of personal memorabilia – even an inscription in a book). Approached in a light-hearted way, for the purpose of entertaining, even something as apparently 'dry' as a collection of memos can reveal narrative, characterisation, and demonstrate reflection.

■ MAKING A START

One of the most accessible subjects for personal writing is a vivid early memory. We all have these. It is a question of selecting and then 'shaping' the memory. You can, of course, alter it; it does not have to be true in every (or any) respect, but you would be advised to start with a genuine memory. At this stage in your life you will have a retrospective view and so are in a position to reflect on it. You may, or may not, choose to do this.

■ Select a vivid early memory (vivid in that it was sad, happy, funny, frightening, whatever). Try to establish for yourself what makes it particularly memorable. Write the account freely. When re-reading it you should check that the event(s) are clear to the reader. (Remember that because it is your own memory it will always be clear to you.) You should also make sure that you have captured the impact of the moment for the reader, the very aspect that made it vivid for you.

It is helpful, when trying to recapture a memory, to concentrate on the senses – particularly the senses of smell and sound. As children we absorb sounds and smells and their associations, almost without being aware of them. So, when these emerge from our subconscious in later life, they can be very evocative and trigger a flood of memories. The skills and craft of narrative writing, discussed in Chapters 2 and 3, will also apply here.

■ If you have not thought of a memory by the end of the last paragraph, think about your first day at school. Surely unforgettable! How are you going to start? Consider the strengths and weaknesses of the following openings:

I shall never forget my first day at school...

I wished my mother hadn't brought me because I knew I was going to cry – and I think she was too...

As soon as I saw Darren in the playground, I knew it was going to be exciting/fun/misery...

The school-room smelt stuffy and the windows were too high up to see out...

And there is the memorable account in Laurie Lee's *Cider with Rosie*:

I arrived at the school just three feet tall and fatly wrapped in my scarves. The playground roared like a rodeo, and the potato burned through my thigh. Old boots, ragged stockings, torn trousers and skirts, went skating and skidding around me. The rabble closed in; I was encircled; grit flew in my face like shrapnel. Tall girls with frizzled hair, and huge boys with sharp elbows, began to prod me with hideous interest. They plucked at my scarves, spun me round like a top, screwed my nose, and stole my potato.

■ When you have written your piece, discuss it with a partner, then make the changes that you think would improve it.

Summary

- personal writing should reveal the individuality of the person or persona
- you should choose an appropriate form for the piece

■ REFLECTIVE WRITING

Where personal writing can differ markedly from the more narrative form is when it becomes mainly reflective. Reflective writing is personal writing of a specific kind. The writer has a chance to present thoughts, objects, ideas, incidents, propositions, whatever, and turn them round in the mind and imagination. It gives the writer the opportunity to examine a topic, a theme, an idea in an individual way. As in life itself, reflection is often prompted by a chance moment, something overheard, a memory, a sound, a perfume – any stimulus to the senses – which then sets in train an imaginative and intellectual process. What happens is the triggering of a chain of thoughts, observations and connections within the writer's own imagination. The artistry lies in creating a coherent and interesting shape from the disparate material so that a focus for the ideas is created, and a recognisable thread emerges for the reader.

Alistair Cooke, who in his broadcast *Letters from America* has made the spoken essay seem natural, unforced, interesting and informative, often has a strongly reflective element in his work. Sometimes the reflection is blended with the informational and the anecdotal, but, generally speaking, it is the reflection that threads the whole piece together.

■ Read *It's a Democracy, Isn't It?* (Section Two, page 104), taken from a selection of Cooke's *Letters from America 1946–1951*. Notice the way he builds up to 'what Americans call democracy' and observe the variety of approaches he makes in reflecting on that theme. Notice also the 'trigger' that sets in train the idea for the piece of writing in the first place.

When you attempt reflective writing it is helpful to re-read as you write to make sure that you are not only recounting something personal, supplying anecdote or illustration, but also that you are significantly reflecting upon this and the contribution it makes to your theme or idea. Keep a running check on this and see where the reflection is taking you. There is always a danger that your writing will connect only with the memories, and not with the reflection.

■ Try a few exercises in the association of ideas as a warm-up for this kind of writing. Start with something evocative, like a smell, a sound, a texture. You will have triggers of your own but here are some suggestions:

fish and chips
paraffin
the sound of the sea
lavender

wood smoke
clean, ironed sheets

Take an idea and run with it; let the associations build. Something on the lines of: paraffin – lamps – soft light – restaurant – argument with the waiter... All of this might lead up to reflection on the difficulty of making complaints without giving offence.

■ MAKING A START

■ Look at photographs **E** and **G** (pages 124 and 126). Allow them to start off a train of thoughts and ideas in your mind. Choose the most promising and then make a few jottings. Consider where these can take you. Now, with the constraints that your notes set, turn over your ideas to make a coherent and reflective thread for the reader. Write freely, and return later to read your work with a critical eye, and make carefully considered changes, particularly to ensure that you have not lost your reflective thread. As well as being coherent and reflective, the piece should allow your individual voice to be heard – it is, after all, *your* reflection.

SUMMARY

■ reflective writing turns round an idea, thought, experience and holds it up to the light
■ the individuality of the thinking and reflective process should emerge

---

7

Conveying Information

Clay pigeon shooting, stamp collecting and growing geraniums are topics that might qualify for 'Write about your hobby'. But there is much more to be explored and experimented with when writing to convey information than might be suggested by this kind of task.

Let us consider the subjective–objective spin on what passes for information. If we buy a pound of carrots and ask the greengrocer the price, we do not expect an answer which prevaricates – 'Well, yesterday they were seventeen pence. Today they might be a little more – I'm not sure yet.' When we read (or watch) a shampoo advertisement we are inclined to suspend belief for most of the claims made for the product. That's part of the game of advertising and we, the target audience, tend to accept the 'rules'. (What makes us actually go out and buy a product as a result of seeing an advertisement is quite complex, and probably has more to do with what we perceive our own needs to be than with belief in the objectivity of the information given.) Market researchers are forever engaged in trying to determine the right balance of truth and fiction that will flatter the consumer into making a purchase without stretching incredulity beyond the point of near belief.

When you have a point or a case to make – in conversation or, more formally, in writing – you marshal your information to make your points as persuasively as possible. You load your information towards your own point of view, belief or particular interest. If, on the other hand, you are a witness giving evidence to the police you are obliged to be as factual and as objective with your information as possible. Even in the gathering and reporting of events the truth–fiction axis is in play. A limited sampling of a range of newspapers will show clearly how elastic is the interpretation of the word 'news' and how different, therefore, will be the reader's interpretation of information. This will be particularly evident in the headlines used. Look at page 134 in Section Two for a selection of headlines on the same topic taken from five 'quality' newspapers of the same date. And look at pages 135–6 in

Section Two for the different 'lines' taken by several newspapers on the same item of news. When conveying information an author must have a clear sense of purpose and audience. In writing to convey your information your purpose is likely to be imagined rather than real.

When writing informatively there are, therefore, certain very important considerations to be made:

> your purpose (real or imagined) in conveying information
> who your readers are
> the quality of the information – how good is it?
> what you feel about the information – do you believe it?
> the medium in which the information is written
> how much bias and emphasis you want to give

In the last six chapters you have been directed to study and note examples of writers practising their craft. It is just as important, in learning and practising the variety of ways in which you can convey information, to read and study examples of writing in this genre. You will find a ready supply of such writing in the 'quality' journals such as *The Times*, *The Guardian*, *The Independent*, *The Observer*, *The Daily Telegraph* and, for those of you in Scotland, *Scotland on Sunday*. Get into the habit of sampling them and reading the material attentively. You should look for the leading articles, editorial comment, main news, articles profiling individuals, as well as travel and food writing. Again, remember to read from a writer's point of view – think about what the writer is trying to achieve; the relationship between writer and reader; the bias or emphasis that the writer gives. You should also try to establish for yourself just how much of any piece of writing in this genre is designed to entertain; how much to inform.

■ WRITING ABOUT A TOPIC

Let us suppose that you intend to write about growing geraniums. You need to know a good deal about the topic. If you don't, then you must do your research. It is also important that you have some kind of relationship to your knowledge on the topic. (You might not actually like growing geraniums and wish to write a humorous piece about geranium growing in order to convey this attitude.) You will have to decide in advance whether you are writing for the general reader or for the informed, enthusiastic reader. Are you writing an essay under the title *Not One of My Pastimes*, a piece for a gardening manual, or an informative snippet to go on a seed packet? All the above considerations will determine the degree of bias – subjectivity or objectivity – with which you approach the topic. They will also determine the tone of the piece, e.g. personal, ironic, humorous.

It is not envisaged that you will be writing a text for a seed packet, but you will be writing to interest, perhaps entertain, as well as to inform, your reader. It is often just as important, therefore, that your individual voice can be heard in this kind of writing as in personal writing. Remember, you are writing as an individual and the informational text with which you are concerned is being crafted by you. The material is yours, in that you can make it the kind of text you want, within whatever constraints are set by the purpose, topic, audience and you yourself. (You are not, in the kinds of writing under consideration in this book, required to write up the notes of a chemistry experiment, however hard a task that is.) Read the extract on dinosaurs taken from David Attenborough's *Life on Earth* (Section Two, page 108) and note the natural voice of the author that emerges.

The best way to start is to choose your own topic, paying attention to the advice, guidelines and warnings given above.

SUMMARY

- when conveying information you must have a clear purpose
- when writing informational texts you need to have the necessary knowledge
- you need to be clear about the audience you are writing for
- you need to know the bias or emphasis that you wish to make
- you need to be clear about the tone you want to set

■ WRITING ARGUMENT

The guidelines given above should also help you when writing argument. In considering the quality of argument, it is necessary also to be concerned with how you marshal the information that supports your argument so that your points are carefully and persuasively presented. Incidentally, do not think that you should only put the case for your own point of view or argument. It is good debating technique to consider opposing views – in order, of course, to reveal their weaknesses, illogicalities and dangers. Listen to the politicians: they will provide you with innumerable examples of this model. Your reading in this genre should alert you to other techniques such as: asking the questions that you intend to answer; giving the readers signposts to help them follow your reasoning; using phrases that show your link to the readers (e.g. 'of course' which you will, incidentally, find in use in this book).

Read Andrew Marr's *Strong tonic for the anaemic body politic* (Section Two, page 111). You will observe that the first paragraph is built on questions, and questions are posed throughout the piece. There is also evidence of opposition:

Yet if Westminster has less and less purchase...

There are signposts to follow:

So far so dandy.

After a year of struggling with it, I was forced back to the basics.

Our system is like this.

And, in several places, phrases are used to link the writer to the readers:

...it hardly needs to be said

But if we are going to take politics seriously...

There are, of course...

■ DISCURSIVE WRITING

This form of writing has its basis in reasoning rather than argument. It is a process of deliberation that allows you to posit theories, to consider information, and to draw conclusions. Remember that you are the writer, and so the choice of issues and the process of 'reasoning' is yours to determine, as are the conclusions. Since you are essentially concerned with writing as art, as something created, your deliberations do not have to have a legal seriousness but should result in a satisfyingly artistic piece, where 'facts', theories, and issues are inspirationally explored and persuasively completed. Good discursive writing, therefore, while it should display reasoned debate and consideration of the issues in question, should also take the reader on a journey of discovery – perhaps even of conversion. Read the extract below by David Hume, the eighteenth century philosopher. It is taken from his *Enquiries Concerning the Human Understanding*, published posthumously in 1777. Hume is here considering Probability.

Though there is no such thing as *Chance* in the world; our ignorance of the real cause of any event has the same influence on the understanding, and begets a like species of belief or opinion.

There is certainly a probability, which arises from a superiority of chances on any side; and according as this superiority increases, and surpasses the opposite chances, the probability receives a proportional increase...If a dye were marked with one figure or number of spots on four sides, and with another figure or number of spots on the remaining two sides, it would be more probable, that the former would turn up than the latter; though if it had a thousand sides marked in the same manner, and only one side different, the probability would be much higher, and our belief or expectation of the event more steady and secure. This process of the thought or reasoning may seem trivial and obvious; but to those who consider it more narrowly, it may, perhaps, afford matter for curious speculation.

It seems evident, that when the mind looks forward to discover the event, which may result from the throw of such a dye, it considers the turning up of each particular side as alike probable; and this is the very nature of chance, to render all the particular events, comprehended in it, entirely equal. But finding a greater number of sides concur in the one event than in the other, the mind is carried more frequently to that event, and meets it oftener, in revolving the various possibilities or chances, on which the ultimate result depends. This concurrence of several views in one particular event begets immediately, by an inexplicable contrivance of nature, the sentiment of belief...

In undertaking discursive writing you will need to be well informed, but you will not necessarily have to be as partisan as to write argument for or against. Indeed, your exploration of a topic is likely to benefit from a degree of objectivity and impartiality (which might, of course, be apparent rather than real). You might, in fact, wish to write from a neutral position (either genuine or convincingly assumed). Again, you might wish to write a humorous or ironic piece.

MAKING A START

Look at Picture **H** (page 127) and then write a piece on *The Quest for Health and Fitness*. (You might want to give the piece 'straight' treatment, or write ironically, humorously, passionately – even scathingly.)

Summary

- when writing argument you should be well informed
- whatever bias you make you should attempt to put both sides of the case – it can help your argument (e.g. in establishing contrast)
- discursive writing should be based on sound information
- it should show reasoning and be convincing in conclusion

■ Giving your writing colour

In all presentation of information it is important to give examples, to make your points more concrete. (Consider Hume's example of the die.) Much of this genre of writing can become too generalised or abstract. Exemplification and illustration will give detail and focus, and will also help to create your own individual voice, since you select the focus. Exemplification can sometimes be made in the form of recommendations to the reader. This might well be part of the technique the writer uses to establish a relationship with the reader in, for instance, travel writing, food writing and literary (and other) criticism. Consider this paragraph from Victor Keegan's article *The Riviera Touch*. (See Section Two, page 113 for further extracts.)

> If you don't [like basking on busy beaches] then try May and June before the French school holidays begin. Or drive westward along the coast road from La Napoule and you will encounter dozens of small beaches and rocky inlets... The corniche cuts its way through the tortuous red rocks of the Esterel towards Miramar. If you see a line of French cars parked by the side of the road, it almost certainly means there is an inlet down below (with steps) popular with the locals, and where you can bathe in relative peace.

■ Using description

Perhaps the easiest aspect of writing to convey information is when the text calls for you to be essentially descriptive. Writing *about* something, someone, some event, somewhere, demands effective description. Food writing, biography, history and travel writing all come into this category. You will find a supply of examples of these genres in the newspapers listed above. In your reading note how the material (the information) is selected and organised. You should also note the effectiveness of descriptive writing in bringing the topic to life for the reader. You will probably find that you respond favourably to the text because the 'voice' of the writer is clearly present. The writer's attitudes to the subject and to the reader are also important, as demonstrated in the Keegan piece referred to above. You might find it interesting, when reading texts like these, to note just how much is 'information' and how much is something else – an anecdote, an aside, a personal touch – that links the writer to the reader.

■ MAKING A START

■ In early attempts at writing of this kind it would be best to start with a modest task such as describing the characteristics/beauties/ advantages/desirability of your favourite place for a holiday. As your confidence increases, you should be able to try a longer piece of travel writing – perhaps describing and giving information about the area or town in which you live, and making personal as well as informed recommendations to the interested reader.

Because this kind of writing can benefit from being personal, remember to create that individual note which will help to bring the place alive for the reader, rather like looking at photographs which feature people as well as views. You can also bring a text like this to life if you include anecdote. This allows the reader to become involved because it sets up a relationship between the writer and the reader, and it still conveys information. Read *Nice work if you can define it* by John Wells (Section Two, page 114). What is Wells writing about – besides food? See note 14, page 65.

SUMMARY

■ informational writing is enlivened by the writer's voice coming through – perhaps in anecdote or in imagery
■ some kinds of informational writing call for well-observed description

---

■ REFLECTIVE WRITING

You will be aware that it is not really possible to categorise discretely the genres of writing. Reflection, discussed earlier in Chapter 6, can also be an effective part of discursive writing; it can be found in argument and in travel writing, particularly if there is a strong element of the personal, from which it follows naturally. An example of this is to be found in the reflective tone in the John Wells piece mentioned above.

■ Look at the article *After the Freedom, Bread* by Neal Ascherson (Section Two, page 116). Think about the quality of information it contains. What kind of relationship does Ascherson establish with you, the reader? How much of Ascherson's own voice reaches you? See note 15, page 65.

A Second Opinion

(1) Here is the second paragraph of Graham Greene's short story *Jubilee*.

> He examined his collar with anxiety; he hadn't been out of doors for more than a
> week, except at the public-house at the corner to eat his morning and evening
> ham roll; and then he always wore an overcoat and a soiled collar.

You might like to consider the added nuances that this very short paragraph
adds to your understanding of the character. Compare it with your own
paragraph, and what you were able to do – and what you intended to do.

(2) This is a panoramic description which sweeps the countryside, rather like a
camera, until it comes to rest on the abbey ruin, then the chancel and, finally, the
upper window. Notice how short that final sentence of the paragraph is. We
have come to a very marked stop here. What expectations are aroused in you?

(3) The author's deliberate revisiting of the description of the setting with
which the story begins creates resonances and echoes, which compel the
reader to think back to the beginning of the novel with its hint of promise:
two ranch hands planning their future. Thus, with the hindsight that the
reader now has, the full impact and irony of the title can be appreciated –
'the best laid plans *of mice and men...*'

(4) These extracts, which refer so clearly to Maurice's blindness, also serve to
give us insights into the feelings of Isabel and Bertie as well as the rather
restrained feelings of Maurice. They contribute to the reader's fuller
understanding of the story – indeed, are essential to it. It is not, of course,
only Maurice's blindness that is being described. Lawrence is creating a close
connection between these three people by means of Maurice's blindness; it is
as if the relationship between the three is filtered through this. And the
tension is almost palpable.

(5) Even in this short extract there is subtlety in the use of dialogue and in the narrative itself. The 'angrily' is reinforced, for the reader, by the dialogue. Notice the disjunction between the two characters which is pointed up in the contrast of dialogue, and then emphasised by 'you people'. The two lines of narrative (*But she wasn't looking at the land, she was looking at the churchyard* and the last two lines of the extract) show an interestingly subtle shift of narrative viewpoint. The first uses the third person narrative; the second gives the old woman's internal voice (in monologue) but still uses the third person.

(6) The woman's response to the child's delight moves the story immediately from light to dark, but also gives us a contrast of character. The woman's experience of life has drained her (and, for her, the chrysanthemums) of delight, and the child's innocent delight points up the woman's loss. The dialogue foreshadows yet another point in the woman's life and experience when chrysanthemums will mark a milestone.

(7) Incidentally, although this very short story has third person narrative, it also offers internal monologue at the end. There is subtlety of technique to be discovered in a close reading of the story.

(8) Notice that the first five paragraphs start with 'I'. What does this contribute to Spark's portrait of the speaker? What else helps to build up the character of the speaker, and the particular 'voice' of the speaker? What about the speaker's language – is it natural? Where does her obsession with cleanliness take her?

(9) Boyd has created quite a complex character in Charlie – but part of the art is to disguise this complexity. How does Charlie make you feel – irritated, sympathetic, sorry, moved? How honest do you find him? Why does he lose his job? Just a few ideas to keep you thinking.

(10) Note, for example, Sybil's early mention of dealing with the laundry that day. Note also the parallel between the guest's death and the dog's illness. There is not a word nor a moment that is wasted in the whole episode: in taking the action forward, in touches of characterisation, and in Basil's desperate and chaotic (though to him logical) attempts to control the relentless inevitability of the unfolding events. All this contributes to the comedy. The important technique to appreciate in this piece is the economy with which the whole is created and which is, to a significant extent, established by the dialogue.

(11) Do you really need help? Think of someone you know who is elderly. Appearance alters with age. What about emotions – even passions?

(12) Consider the symbolic use of 'red' and the poet's ability to draw the reader into the immediacy of the experience by concentrating on the physical, rather than the emotional. In fact, the emotions, the anger and hurt, would seem to be deflected by understatement and by focusing on objects as symbols.

(13) There are so many to consider:

> hunger of blood
> Blue...malice
> thinly drawn
> famishing for flesh
>
> blind, blunt bullet-heads
> nuzzle in the hearts
> fine zinc teeth
> sharpness of grief
>
> teeth seem for laughing
> lurk no claws
> no talons at his heels
> antlers...curls

In some cases the image is sharpened by onomatopoeia or made horrific by contrast – like *nuzzle in the hearts*. Each reader is likely to respond in different ways and to different degrees. You have been asked to think about the impact made on you.

(14) You will notice that Wells not only introduces anecdote in the 'asides' about his wife raising the topic of work, but also introduces a reflective and philosophical tone about the very nature of work. You will notice also how these asides form a kind of counterpoint to the description of, and comment on, the food.

(15) This essay brings together the best in discursive writing. It is well informed but not stuffy; it is reflective, personal and literary. The reader is addressed as an equal; Ascherson brings together and shares with the reader experiences and ideas that most readers would not have.

■ *Section Two* ■

Authors' Texts

■ THE BRIGHT SPADE ■

That winter the gravedigger was the busiest man in the island.

They got the thin harvest in and then the wind squatted in the east, a winter witch, and blew the island gray with her breath.

James of Moss died in the last week of October. Jacob dug his grave and got a bottle of whisky for it from the widow of Moss. This death was not unexpected. James of Moss had been ill with dropsy all summer; he had clung to life like the last tattered leaf on a branch.

The gravedigger had hardly sobered up when he was called to the house of Maria of Graystones. There Maria lay as stiff and pale as a candle. He dug her grave near the wall of the kirk. Maria's nephew gave him a goose.

There was not much food in the island even at the beginning of winter, and the ale was sour and thin.

In early November the laird's youngest son was thrown from his horse at the bridge and broke his neck. 'This will need a deep grave,' said Jacob. He threw up many fine white bones, the laird's ancestors, with his spade. The laird gave him half a guinea, and a dram both before and after the funeral.

Late November and early December brought death to Samuel Ling the fisherman, Jean the wife of Ebenezer of Ness, and the boy with the hare lip from the Quarry. They were all poor people and Jacob got nothing at all for his work but a box of coarse tobacco snuff from Ebenezer of Ness. 'I suppose I'll be glad of somebody to bury me when my time comes,' said Jacob, and sneezed heroically for a month till the snuff was finished.

It was a hard winter, and nobody expected most of the old people and the sickly people to see the spring.

At harvest Kirstie had given birth to a daughter, just three months after she had married Amos of the Glebe. Kirstie and Amos raged at each other so much, both before and after the birth, that there wasn't a bowl or a dish unbroken in the cupboard. In the season of snow and small fires the infant breathed her last; she died the week before Christmas. Jacob dug a small grave in the east corner of the kirkyard. He got a shilling from Kirstie and a pocket-full of potatoes from Amos. The day after the funeral Kirstie left Amos and went back to her parents' house. She never lived with Amos again.

The day after New Year a Dutch ship went ashore at the Red Head. Unfortunately the ship had no cargo; she was in ballast, bound for Labrador. Seven bodies were found on the shore next morning. The minister asked Jacob to dig one large grave for the foreigners.

'Who will pay my fee?' said Jacob.

'I don't know that,' said the minister, 'for the next-of-kin are in the Low Countries.'

In the end Jacob agreed to dig their grave for three spars of timber from the wrecked ship and half a barrel of oil out of the hold.

That month the food was very low in girnal and kirn. Before the beginning of February Abraham of Corse died, and the cripple girl from the Glebe. Jacob got nothing for the girl. The widow of Corse gave him Abraham's brass watch. Abraham was ninety-four years old, and the girl from the Glebe sixteen.

One night there was a meeting in the ale-house. All the men of the island were there. They took counsel together about the impending famine. That same morning the old man of Cornquoy who lived alone, the fiddler, had been found dead in his chair, after he had been missed for a week. They broke down his door. The young dog was gnawing at the corpse's thigh. Jacob got his fiddle the night he shrouded him, though he knew nothing about music. The fiddle, once a sweet brimming shell, hung at Jacob's wall like a shrivelled chrysalis. The old fiddler was as light as a bird to handle. He needed a narrow grave.

'The meal and the meat are done in the island,' said Harald of Ness at the meeting. 'I've eaten nothing myself but a handful of cold potatoes every day for the past week. My suggestion is this, that seven of the strongest men among us cross between the hills to the shore and get a large supply of limpets and dulse from the rocks at low tide.'

The men agreed that it would be necessary to do that.

The seven men chosen set off at dawn the next day. They were Harald of Ness, Adam of Skarataing, Ezekiel of the Burn, Thomas and Philip of Graystones, Simon the blacksmith and Walter of Muce. That same morning the worst blizzard of winter descended, great swirling blankets of snow out of the east. Tinkers saw the seven men between the hills going towards the shore, like a troop of spectres. They were never seen again till their bodies were dug from the drifts a week later.

For the second time that winter Jacob laid seven men together in the kirkyard. This time he would accept no payment at all for his services – 'for,' said he, 'it seems I have done better this winter than anybody else in the island ...'

In March Francis Halcro the coughing sailor who had been with John Paul Jones in the American Wars died at Braebuster. Jacob buried him for his set of Nantucket harpoons.

And then men brought out ploughs, harness, harrows. The implements were dull and rusty after the hard winter. Jacob's spade, on the other hand, was thin and bright with much employment. 'God grant,' he said to the spade, putting it away in his shed, 'that I won't be needing you again till after the shearing and the lobster fishing and the harvest.'

George Mackay Brown

■ THE BLIND MAN ■

Isabel Pervin was listening for two sounds – for the sound of wheels on the drive outside and for the noise of her husband's footsteps in the hall. Her dearest and oldest friend, a man who seemed almost indispensable to her living, would drive up in the rainy dusk of the closing November day. The trap had gone to fetch him from the station. And her husband, who had been blinded in Flanders, and who had a disfiguring mark on his brow, would be coming in from the out-houses.

He had been home for a year now. He was totally blind. Yet they had been very happy. The Grange was Maurice's own place. The back was a farmstead, and the Wernhams, who occupied the rear premises, acted as farmers. Isabel lived with her husband in the handsome rooms in front. She and he had been almost entirely alone together since he was wounded. They talked and sang and read together in a wonderful and unspeakable intimacy. Then she reviewed books for a Scottish newspaper, carrying on her old interest, and he occupied himself a good deal with the farm. Sightless, he could still discuss everything with Wernham, and he could also do a good deal of work about the place – menial work, it is true, but it gave him satisfaction. He milked the cows, carried in the pails, turned the separator, attended to the pigs and horses. Life was still very full and strangely serene for the blind man, peaceful with the almost incomprehensible peace of immediate contact in darkness. With his wife he had a whole world, rich and real and invisible.

They were newly and remotely happy. He did not even regret the loss of his sight in these times of dark, palpable joy. A certain exultance swelled his soul.

But as time wore on, sometimes the rich glamour would leave them. Sometimes, after months of this intensity, a sense of burden overcame Isabel, a weariness, a terrible ennui, in that silent house approached between a colonnade of tall-shafted pines. Then she felt she would go mad, for she could not bear it. And sometimes he had devastating fits of depression, which seemed to lay waste his whole being. It was worse than depression – a black misery, when his own life was a torture to him, and when his presence was unbearable to his wife. The dread went down to the roots of her soul as these black days recurred. In a kind of panic she tried to wrap herself up still further in her husband. She forced the old spontaneous cheerfulness and joy to continue. But the effort it cost her was almost too much. She knew she could not keep it up. She felt she would scream with the strain, and would give anything, anything, to escape. She longed to possess her husband utterly; it gave her inordinate joy to have him entirely to herself. And yet, when again he was gone in a black and massive misery, she could not bear him, she could not bear herself; she wished she could be snatched away off the earth altogether, anything rather than live at this cost.

Dazed, she schemed for a way out. She invited friends, she tried to give him some further connection with the outer world. But it was no good. After all their joy and suffering, after their dark, great year of blindness and solitude and unspeakable nearness, other people seemed to them both shallow, prattling, rather impertinent.

Shallow prattle seemed presumptuous. He became impatient and irritated, she was wearied. And so they lapsed into their solitude again. For they preferred it.

But now, in a few weeks' time, her second baby would be born. The first had died, an infant, when her husband first went out to France. She looked with joy and relief to the coming of the second. It would be her salvation. But also she felt some anxiety. She was thirty years old, her husband was a year younger. They both wanted the child very much. Yet she could not help feeling afraid. She had her husband on her hands, a terrible joy to her, and a terrifying burden. The child would occupy her love and attention. And then, what of Maurice? What would he do? If only she could feel that he, too, would be at peace and happy when the child came! She did so want to luxuriate in a rich, physical satisfaction of maternity. But the man, what would he do? How could she provide for him, how avert those shattering black moods of his, which destroyed them both?

She sighed with fear. But at this time Bertie Reid wrote to Isabel. He was her old friend, a second or third cousin, a Scotsman, as she was a Scotswoman. They had been brought up near to one another, and all her life he had been her friend, like a brother, but better than her own brothers. She loved him – though not in the marrying sense. There was a sort of kinship between them, an affinity. They understood one another instinctively. But Isabel would never have thought of marrying Bertie. It would have seemed like marrying in her own family.

Bertie was a barrister and a man of letters, a Scotsman of the intellectual type, quick, ironical, sentimental, and on his knees before the women he adored but did not want to marry. Maurice Pervin was different. He came of a good old country family – the Grange was not a very great distance from Oxford. He was passionate, sensitive, perhaps over-sensitive, wincing – a big fellow with heavy limbs and a forehead that flushed painfully. For his mind was slow, as if drugged by the strong provincial blood that beat in his veins. He was very sensitive to his own mental slowness, his feelings being quick and acute. So that he was just the opposite to Bertie, whose mind was much quicker that his emotions, which were not so very fine.

From the first the two men did not like each other. Isabel felt that they *ought* to get on together. But they did not. She felt that if only each could have the clue to the other there would be such a rare understanding between them. It did not come off, however. Bertie adopted a slightly ironical attitude, very offensive to Maurice, who returned the Scotch irony with English resentment, a resentment which deepened sometimes into stupid hatred.

This was a little puzzling to Isabel. However, she accepted it in the course of things. Men were made freakish and unreasonable. Therefore, when Maurice was going out to France for the second time, she felt that, for her husband's sake, she must discontinue her friendship with Bertie. She wrote to the barrister to this effect. Bertram Reid simply replied that in this, as in all other matters, he must obey her wishes, if these were indeed her wishes.

For nearly two years nothing had passed between the two friends. Isabel rather gloried in the fact; she had no compunction. She had one great article of faith, which was, that husband and wife should be so important to one another, that the rest of the world simply did not count. She and Maurice were husband and wife. They loved one another. They would have children. Then let everybody and everything else fade into insignificance outside this connubial felicity. She professed herself quite happy and ready to receive Maurice's friends. She was happy and ready: the happy wife, the ready woman in possession. Without knowing why, the friends retired abashed, and came no more. Maurice, of course, took as much satisfaction in this connubial absorption as Isabel did.

He shared in Isabel's literary activities, she cultivated a real interest in agriculture and cattle-raising. For she, being at heart perhaps an emotional enthusiast, always cultivated the practical side of life, and prided herself on her mastery of practical affairs. Thus the husband and wife had spent the five years of their married life. The last had been one of blindness and unspeakable intimacy. And now Isabel felt a great indifference coming over her, a sort of lethargy. She wanted to be allowed to bear her child in peace, to nod by the fire and drift vaguely, physically, from day to day. Maurice was like an ominous thunder-cloud. She had to keep waking up to remember him.

When a little note came from Bertie, asking if he were to put up a tombstone to their dead friendship, and speaking of the real pain he felt on account of her husband's loss of sight, she felt a pang, a fluttering agitation of re-awakening. And she read the letter to Maurice.

'Ask him to come down,' he said.

'Ask Bertie to come here!' she re-echoed.

'Yes – if he wants to.'

Isabel paused for a few moments.

'I know he wants to – he'd only be too glad,' she replied. 'But what about you, Maurice? How would you like it?'

'I should like it.'

'Well – in that case – But I thought you didn't care for him –'

'Oh, I don't know. I might think differently of him now,' the blind man replied. It was rather abstruse to Isabel.

'Well, dear,' she said, 'if you're quite sure –'

'I'm sure enough. Let him come,' said Maurice.

So Bertie was coming, coming this evening, in the November rain and darkness. Isabel was agitated, racked with her old restlessness and indecision. She had always suffered from this pain of doubt, just an agonising sense of uncertainty. It had begun to pass off, in the lethargy of maternity. Now it returned, and she resented it. She struggled as usual to maintain her calm, composed, friendly bearing, a sort of mask she wore over all her body.

A woman had lighted a tall lamp beside the table, and spread the cloth. The long dining-room was dim, with its elegant but rather severe pieces of old furniture. Only the round table glowed softly under the light. It had a rich, beautiful effect. The white cloth glistened and dropped its heavy, pointed lace corners almost to the carpet, the china was old and handsome, creamy-yellow, with a blotched pattern of harsh red and deep blue, the cups large and bell-shaped, the teapot gallant. Isabel looked at it with superficial appreciation.

Her nerves were hurting her. She looked automatically again at the high, uncurtained windows. In the last dusk she could just perceive outside a huge fir tree swaying its boughs: it was as if she thought it rather than saw it. The rain came flying on the window panes. Ah, why had she no peace? These two men, why did they tear at her? Why did they not come – why was there this suspense?

She sat in a lassitude that was really suspense and irritation. Maurice, at least, might come in – there was nothing to keep him out. She rose to her feet. Catching sight of her reflection in a mirror, she glanced at herself with a slight smile of recognition, as if she were an old friend to herself. Her face was oval and calm, her nose a little arched. Her neck made a beautiful line down to her shoulder. With hair knotted loosely behind, she had something of a warm, maternal look. Thinking this of herself, she arched her eyebrows and her rather heavy lids, with a little flicker of a smile, and for a moment her grey eyes looked amused and wicked, a little sardonic, out of her transfigured Madonna face.

Then, resuming her air of womanly patience – she was really fatally self-determined – she went with a little jerk towards the door. Her eyes were slightly reddened.

She passed down the wide hall, and through a door at the end. Then she was in the farm premises. The scent of dairy, and of farm-kitchen, and of farmyard and of leather almost overcame her: but particularly the scent of dairy. They had been scalding out the pans. The flagged passage in front of her was dark, puddled and wet. Light came out from the open kitchen door. She went forward and stood in the doorway. The farm-people were at tea, seated at a little distance from her, round a long, narrow table, in the centre of which stood a white lamp. Ruddy faces, ruddy hands holding food, red mouths working, heads bent over the tea-cups: men, land-girls, boys: it was tea-time, feeding-time. Some faces caught sight of her. Mrs. Wernham, going round behind the chairs with a large black teapot, halting slightly in her walk, was not aware of her for a moment. Then she turned suddenly.

'Oh, is it Madame!' she exclaimed. 'Come in, then, come in! We're at tea.' And she dragged forward a chair.

'No, I won't come in,' said Isabel. 'I'm afraid I interrupt your meal.'

'No – no – not likely, Madame, not likely.'

'Hasn't Mr. Pervin come in, do you know?'

'I'm sure I couldn't say! Missed him have you, Madame?'

'No, I only wanted him to come in,' laughed Isabel, as if shyly.

'Wanted him, did ye? Get up, boy – get up, now –'

Mrs. Wernham knocked one of the boys on the shoulder. He began to scrape to his feet, chewing largely.

'I believe he's in top stable,' said another voice from the table.

'Ah! No, don't get up. I'm going myself,' said Isabel.

'Don't you go out of a dirty night like this. Let the lad go. Get along wi' ye, boy,' said Mrs. Wernham.

'No, no,' said Isabel, with a decision that was always obeyed. 'Go on with your tea, Tom. I'd like to go across to the stable, Mrs. Wernham.'

'Did ever you hear tell!' exclaimed the woman.

'Isn't the trap late?' asked Isabel.

'Why, no,' said Mrs. Wernham, peering into the distance at the tall, dim clock. 'No, Madame – we can give it another quarter or twenty minutes yet, good – yes, every bit of a quarter.'

'Ah! It seems late when darkness falls so early,' said Isabel.

'It do, that it do. Bother the days, that they draw in so,' answered Mrs. Wernham. 'Proper miserable!'

'They are,' said Isabel, withdrawing.

She pulled on her overshoes, wrapped a large tartan shawl around her, put on a man's felt hat, and ventured out along the causeways of the first yard. It was very dark. The wind was roaring in the great elms behind the out-houses. When she came to the second yard the darkness seemed deeper. She was unsure of her footing. She wished she had brought a lantern. Rain blew against her. Half she liked it, half she felt unwilling to battle.

She reached at last the just visible door of the stable. There was no sign of a light anywhere. Opening the upper half, she looked in: into a simple well of darkness. The smell of horses, ammonia, and of warmth was startling to her, in that full night. She listened with all her ears, but could hear nothing save the night, and the stirring of a horse.

'Maurice!' she called, softly and musically, though she was afraid. 'Maurice – are you there?'

Nothing came from the darkness. She knew the rain and wind blew in upon the horses, the hot animal life. Feeling it wrong, she entered the stable, and drew the lower half of the door shut, holding the upper part close. She did not stir, because she was aware of the presence of the dark hindquarters of the horses, though she could not see them, and she was afraid. Something wild stirred in her heart.

She listened intensely. Then she heard a small noise in the distance – far away, it seemed – the chink of a pan, and a man's voice speaking a brief word. It would be Maurice, in the other part of the stable. She stood motionless, waiting for him to come through the partition door. The horses were so terrifyingly near to her, in the invisible.

The loud jarring of the inner door-latch made her start; the door was opened. She could hear and feel her husband entering and invisibly passing among the horses near to her, in the darkness as they were, actively intermingled. The rather low sound of his voice as he spoke to the horses came velvety to her nerves. How near he was, and how invisible! The darkness seemed to be in a strange swirl of violent life, just upon her. She turned giddy.

Her presence of mind made her call, quietly and musically:

'Maurice! Maurice – dea-ar!'

'Yes,' he answered. 'Isabel?'

She saw nothing, and the sound of his voice seemed to touch her.

'Hello!' she answered cheerfully, straining her eyes to see him. He was still busy, attending to the horses near her, but she saw only darkness. It made her almost desperate.

'Won't you come in, dear?' she said.

'Yes, I'm coming. Just half a minute. *Stand over – now!* Trap's not come, has it?'

'Not yet,' said Isabel.

His voice was pleasant and ordinary, but it had a slight suggestion of the stable to her. She wished he would come away. While he was so utterly invisible she was afraid of him.

'How's the time,' he asked.

'Not yet six,' she replied. She disliked to answer into the dark. Presently he came very near to her, and she retreated out of doors.

'The weather blows in here,' he said, coming steadily forward, feeling for the doors. She shrank away. At last she could dimly see him.

'Bertie won't have much of a drive,' he said, as he closed the doors.

'He won't indeed!' said Isabel calmly, watching the dark shape at the door.

'Give me your arm, dear,' she said.

She pressed his arm close to her, as she went. But she longed to see him, to look at him. She was nervous. He walked erect, with face rather lifted, but with a curious tentative movement of his powerful, muscular legs. She could feel the clever, careful, strong contact of his feet with the earth, as she balanced against him. For a moment he was a tower of darkness to her, as if he rose out of the earth.

In the house-passage he wavered, and went cautiously, with a curious look of silence about him as he felt for the bench. Then he sat down heavily. He was a man with rather sloping shoulders, but with heavy limbs, powerful legs that seemed to know the earth. His head was small, usually carried high and light. As he bent down to unfasten his gaiters and boots he did not look blind. His hair was brown and crisp, his hands were large, reddish, intelligent, the veins stood out in the wrists; and his thighs and knees seemed massive. When he stood up his face and neck were surcharged with blood, the veins stood out on his temples. She did not look at his blindness.

Isabel was always glad when they had passed through the dividing door into their own regions of repose and beauty. She was a little afraid of him, out there in the animal grossness of the back. His bearing also changed, as he smelt the familiar, indefinable odour that pervaded his wife's surroundings, a delicate, refined scent, very faintly spicy. Perhaps it came from the pot-pourri bowls.

He stood at the foot of the stairs, arrested, listening. She watched him, and her heart sickened. He seemed to be listening to fate.

'He's not here yet,' he said. 'I'll go up and change.'

'Maurice,' she said, 'you're not wishing he wouldn't come, are you?'

'I couldn't quite say,' he answered. 'I feel myself rather on the *qui vive*.'

'I can see you are,' she answered. And she reached up and kissed his cheek. She saw his mouth relax into a slow smile.

'What are you laughing at?' she said roguishly.

'You consoling me,' he answered.

'Nay,' she answered. 'Why should I console you? You know we love each other – you know *how* married we are! What does anything else matter?'

'Nothing at all, my dear.'

He felt for her face, and touched it, smiling.

'*You're* all right, aren't you?' he asked, anxiously.

'I'm wonderfully all right, love,' she answered. 'It's you I am a little troubled about, at times.'

'Why me?' he said, touching her cheeks delicately with the tips of his fingers. The touch had an almost hypnotising effect on her.

He went away upstairs. She saw him mount into the darkness, unseeing and unchanging. He did not know that the lamps on the upper corridor were unlighted. He went on into the darkness with unchanging step. She heard him in the bathroom.

Pervin moved about almost unconsciously in his familiar surroundings, dark though everything was. He seemed to know the presence of objects before he touched them. It was a pleasure to him to rock thus through a world of things, carried on the flood in a sort of blood-prescience. He did not think much or trouble much. So long as he kept this sheer immediacy of blood-contact with the substantial world he was happy, he wanted no intervention of visual consciousness. In this state there was a certain rich positivity, bordering sometimes on rapture. Life seemed to move in him like a tide lapping, lapping, and advancing, enveloping all things darkly. It was a pleasure to stretch forth the hand and meet the unseen object, clasp it, and possess it in pure contact. He did not try to remember, to visualise. He did not want to. The new way of consciousness substituted itself in him.

The rich suffusion of this state generally kept him happy, reaching its culmination in the consuming passion for his wife. But at times the flow would seem to be checked and thrown back. Then it would beat inside him like a tangled sea, and he was tortured in the shattered chaos of his own blood. He grew to dread this arrest, this throw-back, this chaos inside himself, when he seemed merely at the mercy of his own powerful and conflicting elements. How to get some measure of control or surety, this was the question. And when the question rose maddening in him, he would clench his fists as if he would *compel* the whole universe to submit to him. But it was in vain. He could not even compel himself.

To-night, however, he was still serene, though little tremors of unreasonable exasperation ran through him. He had to handle the razor very carefully, as he shaved, for it was not at one with him, he was afraid of it. His hearing also was too much sharpened. He heard the woman lighting the lamps on the corridor, and attending to the fire in the visitor's room. And then, as he went to his room he heard the trap arrive. Then came Isabel's voice, lifted and calling, like a bell ringing:

'Is it you, Bertie? Have you come?'

And a man's voice answered out of the wind:

'Hullo, Isabel! There you are.'

'Have you had a miserable drive? I'm so sorry we couldn't send a closed carriage. I can't see you at all you know.'

'I'm coming. No, I liked the drive – it was like Perthshire. Well, how are you? You're looking fit as ever, as far as I can see.'

'Oh, yes,' said Isabel. 'I'm wonderfully well. How are you? Rather thin, I think –'

'Worked to death – everybody's old cry. But I'm all right, Ciss. How's Pervin? – isn't he here?'

'Oh, yes, he's upstairs changing. Yes, he's awfully well. Take off your wet things; I'll send them to be dried.'

'And how are you both, in spirits? He doesn't fret?'

'No – no, not at all. No, on the contrary, really. We've been wonderfully happy, incredibly. It's more than I can understand – so wonderful: the nearness, and the peace –'

'Ah! Well, that's awfully good news –'

They moved away. Pervin heard no more. But a childish sense of desolation had come over him, as he heard their brisk voices. He seemed shut out – like a child that is left out. He was aimless and excluded, he did not know what to do with himself. The helpless desolation came over him. He fumbled nervously as he dressed himself, in a state almost of childishness. He disliked the Scotch accent in Bertie's speech, and the slight response it found on Isabel's tongue. He disliked the slight purr of complacency in the Scottish speech. He disliked intensely the glib way in which Isabel spoke of their happiness and nearness. It made him recoil. He was fretful and beside himself like a child, he had almost a childish nostalgia to be included in the life circle. And at the same time he was a man, dark and powerful and infuriated by his own weakness. By some fatal flaw, he could not be by himself, he had to depend on the support of another. And this very dependence enraged him. He hated Bertie Reid, and at the same time he knew the hatred was nonsense, he knew it was the outcome of his own weakness.

He went downstairs. Isabel was alone in the dining-room. She watched him enter, head erect, his feet tentative. He looked so strong-blooded and healthy, and, at the same time, cancelled. Cancelled – that was the word that flew across her mind. Perhaps it was his scars suggested it.

'You heard Bertie come, Maurice?' she said.

'Yes – isn't he here?'

'He's in his room. He looks very thin and worn.' 'I suppose he works himself to death.'

A woman came in with a tray – and after a few minutes Bertie came down. He was a little dark man, with a very big forehead, thin, wispy hair, and sad, large eyes. His expression was inordinately sad – almost funny. He had odd, short legs.

Isabel watched him hesitate under the door and glance nervously at her husband. Pervin heard him and turned.

'Here you are, now,' said Isabel. 'Come, let us eat.'

Bertie went across to Maurice.

'How are you, Pervin?' he said, as he advanced.

The blind man stuck his hand out into space, and Bertie took it.

'Very fit. Glad you've come,' said Maurice.

Isabel glanced at them, and glanced away, as if she could not bear to see them.

'Come,' she said. 'Come to table. Aren't you both awfully hungry? I am, tremendously.'

'I'm afraid you waited for me,' said Bertie, as they sat down.

Maurice had a curious monolithic way of sitting in a chair, erect and distant. Isabel's heart always beat when she caught sight of him thus.

'No,' she replied to Bertie. 'We're very little later than usual. We're having a sort of high tea, not dinner. Do you mind? It gives us such a nice long evening uninterrupted.'

'I like it,' said Bertie.

Maurice was feeling, with curious little movements, almost like a cat kneading her bed, for his place, his knife and his fork, his napkin. He was getting the whole geography of his cover into his consciousness. He sat erect and inscrutable, remote-seeming. Bertie watched the static figure of the blind man, the delicate tactile discernment of the large, ruddy hands, and the curious mindless silence of the brow, above the scar. With difficulty he looked away, and without knowing what he did, picked up a little crystal bowl of violets from the table, and held them to his nose.

'They are sweet-scented,' he said. 'Where do they come from?'

'From the garden – under the windows,' said Isabel.

'So late in the year – and so fragrant! Do you remember the violets under Aunt Bell's south wall?'

The two friends looked at each other and exchanged a smile, Isabel's eyes lighting up.

'Don't I?' she replied. '*Wasn't* she queer!'

'A curious old girl,' laughed Bertie. 'There's a streak of freakishness in the family, Isabel.'

'Ah – but not in you and me, Bertie,' said Isabel. 'Give them to Maurice, will you?' she added, as Bertie was putting down the flowers. 'Have you smelled the violets, dear? Do! – they are so scented.'

Maurice held out his hand, and Bertie placed the tiny bowl against his large, warm-looking fingers. Maurice's hand closed over the thin white fingers of the barrister. Bertie carefully extricated himself. Then the two watched the blind man smelling the violets. He bent his head and seemed to be thinking. Isabel waited.

'Aren't they sweet, Maurice?' she said at last, anxiously.

'Very,' he said. And he held out the bowl. Bertie took it. Both he and Isabel were a little afraid, and deeply disturbed.

The meal continued. Isabel and Bertie chatted spasmodically. The blind man was silent. He touched his food repeatedly, with quick, delicate touches of his knife-point, then cut irregular bits. He could not bear to be helped. Both Isabel and Bertie suffered: Isabel wondered why. She did not suffer when she was alone with Maurice. Bertie made her conscious of a strangeness.

After the meal the three drew their chairs to the fire, and sat down to talk. The decanters were put on a table near at hand. Isabel knocked the logs on the fire, and clouds of brilliant sparks went up the chimney. Bertie noticed a slight weariness in her bearing.

'You will be glad when your child comes now, Isabel?' he said.

She looked up to him with a quick wan smile.

'Yes, I shall be glad,' she answered. 'It begins to seem long. Yes, I shall be very glad. So will you, Maurice, won't you?' she added.

'Yes, I shall,' replied her husband.

'We are both looking forward so much to having it,' she said.

'Yes, of course,' said Bertie.

He was a bachelor, three or four years older than Isabel. He lived in beautiful rooms overlooking the river, guarded by a faithful Scottish manservant. And he had his friends amongst the fair sex – not lovers, friends. So long as he could avoid any danger of courtship or marriage, he adored a few good women with constant and unfailing homage, and he was chivalrously fond of quite a number. But if they seemed to encroach on him, he withdrew and detested them.

Isabel knew him very well, knew his beautiful constancy, and kindness, also his incurable weakness, which made him unable ever to enter into close contact of any sort. He was ashamed of himself, because he could not marry, could not approach women physically. He wanted to do so. But he could not. At the centre of him he was afraid, helplessly and even brutally afraid. He had given up hope, had ceased to expect any more that he could escape his own weakness. Hence he was a brilliant and successful barrister, also *littérateur* of high repute, a rich man, and a great social success. At the centre he felt himself neuter, nothing.

Isabel knew him well. She despised him even while she admired him. She looked at his sad face, his little short legs, and felt contempt of him. She looked at his dark grey eyes, with their uncanny, almost childlike intuition, and she loved him. He understood amazingly – but she had no fear of his understanding. As a man she patronised him.

And she turned to the impassive, silent figure of her husband. He sat leaning back, with folded arms, and face a little uptilted. His knees were straight and massive. She sighed, picked up the poker, and again began to prod the fire, to rouse the clouds of soft, brilliant sparks.

'Isabel tells me,' Bertie began suddenly, 'that you have not suffered unbearably from the loss of sight.'

Maurice straightened himself to attend, but kept his arms folded.

'No,' he said, 'not unbearably. Now and again one struggles against it, you know. But there are compensations.'

'They say it is much worse to be stone deaf,' said Isabel.

'I believe it is,' said Bertie. 'Are there compensations?' he added, to Maurice.

'Yes. You cease to bother about a great many things.' Again Maurice stretched his figure, stretched the strong muscles of his back, and leaned backwards, with uplifted face.

'And that is a relief,' said Bertie. But what is there in place of the bothering? What replaces the activity?'

There was a pause. At length the blind man replied, as out of a negligent, unattentive thinking:

'Oh, I don't know. There's a good deal when you're not active.'

'Is there?' said Bertie. 'What, exactly? It always seems to me that when there is no thought and no action, there is nothing.'

Again Maurice was slow in replying.

'There is something,' he replied. 'I couldn't tell you what it is.'

And the talk lapsed once more, Isabel and Bertie chatting gossip and reminiscence, the blind man silent.

At length Maurice rose restlessly, a big, obtrusive figure. He felt tight and hampered. He wanted to go away.

'Do you mind,' he said, 'if I go and speak to Wernham?'

'No – go along, dear,' said Isabel.

And he went out. A silence came over the two friends. At length Bertie said:

'Nevertheless, it is a great deprivation, Cissie.'

'It is, Bertie. I know it is.'

'Something lacking all the time,' said Bertie.

'Yes, I know. And yet – and yet – Maurice is right. There is something else, something *there*, which you never knew was there, and which you can't express.'

'What is there?' asked Bertie.

'I don't know – it's awfully hard to define it – but something strong and immediate. There's something strange in Maurice's presence – indefinable – but I couldn't do without it. I agree that it seems to put one's mind to sleep. But when we're alone I miss nothing; it seems awfully rich, almost splendid, you know.'

'I'm afraid I don't follow,' said Bertie.

They talked desultorily. The wind blew loudly outside, rain chattered on the window-panes, making a sharp drum-sound, because of the closed, mellow-golden shutters inside. The logs burned slowly, with hot, almost invisible small flames. Bertie seemed uneasy, there were dark circles round his eyes. Isabel, rich with her approaching maternity, leaned looking into the fire. Her hair curled in odd, loose strands, very pleasing to the man. But she had a curious feeling of old woe in her heart, old, timeless night-woe.

'I suppose we're all deficient somewhere,' said Bertie.

'I suppose so,' said Isabel wearily.

'Damned, sooner or later.'

'I don't know,' she said, rousing herself. 'I feel quite all right, you know. The child coming seems to make me indifferent to everything, just placid. I can't feel that there's anything to trouble about, you know.'

'A good thing, I should say,' he replied slowly.

'Well, there it is. I suppose it's just Nature. If only I felt I needn't trouble about Maurice, I should be perfectly content –'

'But you feel you must trouble about him?'

'Well – I don't know –' she even resented this much effort.

The evening passed slowly. Isabel looked at the clock. 'I say,' she said. 'It's nearly ten o'clock. Where can Maurice be? I'm sure they're all in bed at the back. Excuse me a moment.'

She went out, returning almost immediately.

'It's all shut up and in darkness,' she said. 'I wonder where he is. He must have gone out to the farm –'

Bertie looked at her.

'I suppose he'll come in,' he said.

'I suppose so,' she said. 'But it's unusual for him to be out now.'

'Would you like me to go out and see?'

'Well – if you wouldn't mind. I'd go, but –' She did not want to make the physical effort.

Bertie put on an old overcoat and took a lantern. He went out from the side door. He shrank from the wet and roaring night. Such weather had a nervous effect on him: too much moisture everywhere made him feel almost imbecile. Unwilling, he went through it all. A dog barked violently at him. He peered in all the buildings. At last, he opened the upper door of a sort of intermediate barn, he heard a grinding noise, and looking in, holding up his lantern, saw Maurice, in his shirt-sleeves, standing listening, holding the handle of a turnip-pulper. He had been pulping sweet roots, a pile of which lay dimly heaped in a corner behind him.

'That you, Wernham? said Maurice, listening.

'No, it's me,' said Bertie.

A large, half-wild grey cat was rubbing at Maurice's leg. The blind man stooped to rub its sides. Bertie watched the scene, then unconsciously entered and shut the door behind him. He was in a high sort of barn-place, from which, right and left, ran off the corridors in front of the stalled cattle. He watched the slow, stooping motion of the other man, as he caressed the great cat.

Maurice straightened himself.

'You came to look for me?' he said.

'Isabel was a little uneasy,' said Bertie.

'I'll come in. I like messing about doing these jobs.'

The cat had reared her sinister, feline length against his leg, clawing at his thigh affectionately. He lifted her claws out of his flesh.

'I hope I'm not in your way at all at the Grange here,' said Bertie, rather shy and stiff.

'My way? No, not a bit. I'm glad Isabel had somebody to talk to. I'm afraid it's I who am in the way. I know I'm not very lively company. Isabel's all right, don't you think? She's not unhappy, is she?'

'I don't think so.'

'What does she say?'

'She says she's very content – only a little troubled about you.'

'Why me?'

'Perhaps afraid that you might brood,' said Bertie cautiously.

'She needn't be afraid of that,' He continued to caress the flattened grey head of the cat with his fingers. 'What I am a bit afraid of,' he resumed, 'is that she'll find me a dead weight, always along with me down here.'

'I don't think you need think that,' said Bertie, though this was what he feared himself.

79

'I don't know,' said Maurice. 'Sometimes I feel it isn't fair that she's saddled with me.' Then he dropped his voice curiously. 'I say,' he asked, secretly struggling, 'is my face much disfigured? Do you mind telling me?'

'There is the scar,' said Bertie, wondering. 'Yes, it is a disfigurement. But more pitiable than shocking,'

'A pretty bad scar, though,' said Maurice.

'Oh yes.'

There was a pause.

'Sometimes I feel I am horrible,' said Maurice, in a low voice, talking as if to himself. And Bertie actually felt a quiver of horror.

'That's nonsense,' he said.

Maurice again straightened himself, leaving the cat.

'There's no telling,' he said. Then again, in an odd tone, he added: 'I don't really know you, do I?'

'Probably not,' said Bertie.

'Do you mind if I touch you?'

The lawyer shrank away instinctively. And yet, out of very philanthropy, he said, in a small voice: 'Not at all.'

But he suffered as the blind man stretched out a strong, naked hand to him. Maurice accidentally knocked off Bertie's hat.

'I thought you were taller,' he said, starting. Then he laid his hand on Bertie Reid's head, closing the dome of the skull in a soft, firm grasp, gathering it, as it were; then, shifting his grasp and softly closing again, with a fine, close pressure, till he had covered the skull and the face of the smaller man, tracing the brows, and touching the full, closed eyes, touching the small nose and the nostrils, the rough, short moustache, the mouth, the rather strong chin. The hand of the blind man grasped the shoulder, the arm, the hand of the other man. He seemed to take him, in the soft, travelling grasp.

'You seem young,' he said quietly, at last.

The lawyer stood almost annihilated, unable to answer.

'Your head seems tender, as if you were young,' Maurice repeated. 'So do your hands. Touch my eyes, will you? – touch my scar.'

Now Bertie quivered with revulsion. Yet he was under the power of the blind man, as if hypnotised. He lifted his hand, and laid the fingers on the scar, on the scarred eyes. Maurice suddenly covered them with his own hand, pressed the fingers of the other man upon his disfigured eye-sockets, trembling in every fibre, and rocking slightly, slowly, from side to side. He remained thus for a minute or more, whilst Bertie stood as if in a swoon, unconscious, imprisoned.

Then suddenly Maurice removed the hand of the other man from his brow, and stood holding it in his own.

'Oh, my God,' he said, 'we shall know each other now, shan't we? We shall know each other now.'

Bertie could not answer. He gazed mute and terror-struck, overcome by his own weakness. He knew he could not answer. He had an unreasonable fear, lest the

)ther man should suddenly destroy him. Whereas Maurice was actually filled with
1ot, poignant love, the passion of friendship. Perhaps it was this very passion of
riendship which Bertie shrank from most.

'We're all right together now, aren't we?' said Maurice. 'It's all right now, as long
1s we live, so far as we're concerned.'

'Yes,' said Bertie, trying by any means to escape.

Maurice stood with head lifted, as if listening. The new delicate fulfilment of
mortal friendship had come as a revelation and surprise to him, something exquisite
1nd unhoped-for. He seemed to be listening to hear if it were real.

Then he turned for his coat.

'Come,' he said, 'we'll go to Isabel.'

Bertie took the lantern and opened the door. The cat disappeared. The two men
went in silence along the causeways. Isabel, as they came, thought their footsteps
5ounded strange. She looked up pathetically and anxiously for their entrance. There
5eemed a curious elation about Maurice. Bertie was haggard, with sunken eyes.

'What is it?' she asked.

'We've become friends,' said Maurice, standing with his feet apart, like a strange
colossus.

'Friends!' re-echoed Isabel. And she looked again at Bertie. He met her eyes with
a furtive, haggard look; his eyes were as if glazed with misery.

'I'm so glad,' she said, in sheer perplexity.

'Yes,' said Maurice.

He was indeed so glad. Isabel took his hand with both hers, and held it fast.

'You'll be happier now, dear,' she said.

But she was watching Bertie. She knew that he had one desire – to escape from
this intimacy, this friendship, which had been thrust upon him. He could not bear it
that he had been touched by the blind man, his insane reserve broken in. He was
like a mollusc whose shell is broken.

D. H. Lawrence

■ A CLEAN, WELL-LIGHTED PLACE ■

It was late and everyone had left the café except an old man who sat in the shadow
the leaves of the tree made against the electric light. In the daytime the street was
dusty, but at night the dew settled the dust and the old man liked to sit late because
he was deaf and now at night it was quiet and he felt the difference. The two
waiters inside the café knew that the old man was a little drunk, and while he was a
good client they knew that if he became too drunk he would leave without paying,
so they kept watch on him.

'Last week he tried to commit suicide,' one waiter said.

'Why?'

'He was in despair.'

'What about?'

'Nothing.'

'How do you know it was nothing?'

'He has plenty of money.'

They sat together at a table that was close against the wall near the door of the café and looked at the terrace where the tables were all empty except where the old man sat in the shadow of the leaves of the tree that moved slightly in the wind. A girl and a soldier went by in the street. The street light shone on the brass number on his collar. The girl wore no head covering and hurried beside him.

'The guard will pick him up,' one waiter said.

'What does it matter if he gets what he's after?'

'He had better get off the street now. The guard will get him. They went by five minutes ago.'

The old man sitting in the shadow rapped on his saucer with his glass. The younger waiter went over to him.

'What do you want?'

The old man looked at him. 'Another brandy,' he said.

'You'll be drunk,' the waiter said. The old man looked at him. The waiter went away.

'He'll stay all night,' he said to his colleague. 'I'm sleepy now. I never get to bed before three o'clock. He should have killed himself last week.'

The waiter took the brandy bottle and another saucer from the counter inside the café and marched out to the old man's table. He put down the saucer and poured the glass full of brandy.

'You should have killed yourself last week,' he said to the deaf man. The old man motioned with his finger. 'A little more,' he said. The waiter poured on into the glass so that the brandy slopped over and ran down the stem into the top saucer of the pile. 'Thank you,' the old man said. The waiter took the bottle back inside the café. He sat down at the table with his colleague again.

'He's drunk now,' he said.

'He's drunk every night.'

'What did he want to kill himself for?'

'How should I know?'

'How did he do it?'

'He hung himself with a rope.'

'Who cut him down?'

'His niece.'

'Why did they do it?'

'Fear for his soul.'

'How much money has he got?'

'He's got plenty.'

'He must be eighty years old.'

'Anyway I should say he was eighty.'

'I wish he would go home. I never get to bed before three o'clock. What kind of hour is that to go to bed?'

'He stays up because he likes it.'

'He's lonely. I'm not lonely. I have a wife waiting in bed for me.'

'He had a wife once too.'

'A wife would be no good to him now.'

'You can't tell. He might be better with a wife.'

'His niece looks after him.'

'I know. You said she cut him down.'

'I wouldn't want to be that old. An old man is a nasty thing.'

'Not always. This old man is clean. He drinks without spilling. Even now, drunk. Look at him.'

'I don't want to look at him. I wish he would go home. He has no regard for those who must work.'

The old man looked from his glass across the square, then over at the waiters.

'Another brandy,' he said, pointing to his glass. The waiter who was in a hurry came over.

'Finished,' he said, speaking with that omission of syntax stupid people employ when talking to drunken people or foreigners. 'No more tonight. Close now.'

'Another,' said the old man.

'No. Finished.' The waiter wiped the edge of the table with a towel and shook his head.

The old man stood up, slowly counted the saucers, took a leather coin purse from his pocket and paid for the drinks, leaving half a peseta tip.

The waiter watched him go down the street, a very old man walking unsteadily but with dignity.

'Why didn't you let him stay and drink?' the unhurried waiter asked. They were putting up the shutters. 'It is not half past two.'

'I want to go home to bed.'

'What is an hour?'

'More to me than to him.'

'An hour is the same.'

'You talk like an old man yourself. He can buy a bottle and drink at home.'

'It's not the same.'

'No, it is not,' agreed the waiter with a wife. He did not wish to be unjust. He was only in a hurry.

'And you? You have no fear of going home before your usual hour?'

'Are you trying to insult me?'

'No, hombre, only to make a joke.'

'No,' the waiter who was in a hurry said, rising from pulling down the metal shutters. 'I have confidence. I am all confidence.'

'You have youth, confidence, and a job,' the older waiter said. 'You have everything.'

'And what do you lack?'

'Everything but work.'

'You have everything I have.'

'No. I have never had confidence and I am not young.'

'Come on. Stop talking nonsense and lock up.'

'I am of those who like to stay late at the café,' the older waiter said. 'With all those who do not want to go to bed. With all those who need a light for the night.'

'I want to go home and into bed.'

'We are of two different kinds,' the older waiter said. He was dressed now to go home. 'It is not only a question of youth and confidence, although those things are very beautiful. Each night I am reluctant to close up because there may be someone who needs the café.'

'Hombre, there are bodegas open all night long.'

'You do not understand. This is a clean and pleasant café. It is well lighted. The light is very good and also, now, there are shadows of leaves.'

'Good night,' said the younger waiter.

'Good night,' the other said. Turning off the electric light he continued the conversation with himself. It is the light of course but it is necessary that the place be clean and pleasant. You do not want music. Certainly you do not want music. Nor can you stand before a bar with dignity although that is all that is provided for these hours. What did he fear? It was not fear or dread. It was a nothing that he knew too well. It was all a nothing and a man was nothing too. It was only that and light was all it needed and a certain cleanness and order. Some lived in it and never felt it but he knew it all was nada y pues nada y nada y pues nada. Our nada who art in nada, nada be thy name thy kingdom nada thy will be nada in nada as it is in nada. Give us this nada our daily nada and nada us our nada as we nada our nadas and nada us not into nada but deliver us from nada; pues nada. Hail nothing full of nothing, nothing is with thee. He smiled and stood before a bar with a shining steam pressure coffee machine.

'What's yours?' asked the barman.

'Nada.'

'Otro loco mas,' said the barman and turned away.

'A little cup,' said the waiter.

The barman poured it for him.

'The light is very bright and pleasant but the bar is unpolished,' the waiter said.

The barman looked at him but did not answer. It was too late at night for conversation.

'You want another copita?' the barman asked.

'No, thank you,' said the waiter and went out. He disliked bars and bodegas. A clean, well-lighted café was a very different thing. Now, without thinking further, he would go home to his room. He would lie in the bed and finally, with daylight, he would go to sleep. After all, he said to himself, it is probably only insomnia. Many must have it.

Ernest Hemingway

■ NOT YET, JAYETTE ■

This happened to me in L.A. once. Honestly. I was standing at a hamburger kiosk on Echo Park eating a chilé-dog. This guy in a dark green Lincoln pulls up at the kerb in front of me and leans out of the window. 'Hey,' he asks me, 'do you know the way to San José?' Well, that threw me, I had to admit it. In fact I almost told him. Then I got wise. 'Don't tell me,' I says. 'Let me guess. You're going back to find some peace of mind.' I only tell you this to give you some idea of what the city is like. It's full of jokers. And that guy, even though I'd figured him, still bad-mouthed me before he drove away. That's the kind of place it is. I'm just telling you so's you know my day is for real.

Most mornings, early, I go down to the beach at Santa Monica to try and meet Christopher Isherwood. A guy I know told me he likes to walk his dog down there before the beach freaks and the surfers show up. I haven't seen him yet but I've grown to like my mornings on the beach. The sea has that oily sheen to it, like an empty swimming pool. The funny thing is, though, the Pacific Ocean nearly always looks cold. One morning someone was swinging on the bars, up and down, flinging himself about as if he was made of rubber. It was beautiful, and boy, was he built. It's wonderful to me what the human body can achieve if you treat it right. I like to keep in shape. I work out. So most days I hang around waiting to see if Christopher's going to show then I go jogging. I head south; down from the pier to Pacific Ocean Park. I've got to know some of the bums that live around the beach, the junkies and derelicts. 'Hi Charlie,' they shout when they see me jogging by.

There's a café in Venice where I eat breakfast. A girl works there most mornings, thin, bottle-blonde, kind of tired-looking. I'm pretty sure she's on something heavy. So that doesn't make her anything special but she can't be more than eighteen. She knows my name, I don't know how, I never told her. Anyway each morning when she brings me my coffee and doughnut she says 'Hi there, Charlie. Lucked-out yet?' I just smile and say 'Not yet, Jayette.' Jayette's the name she's got sewn across her left tit. I'm not sure I like the way she speaks to me – I don't exactly know what she's referring to. But seeing how she knows my name I think it must be my career she's talking about. Because I used to be a star, well, a TV star anyway. Between the ages of nine and eleven I earned twelve thousand dollars a week. Perhaps you remember the show, a TV soap opera called 'The Scrantons'. I was the little brother, Chuck. For two years I was a star. I got the whole treatment: my own trailer, chauffeured limousines, private tutors. Trouble was my puberty came too early. Suddenly I was like a teenage gatecrasher at a kids' party. My voice went, I got zitz all over my chin, fluff on my lip. It spoilt everything. Within a month the scenario for my contractual death was drawn up. I think it was pneumonia, or maybe an accident with the thresher. I can't really remember, I don't like to look back on those final days.

Though I must confess it was fun meeting all the stars. The big ones: Jeanne Lamont, Eddy Cornelle, Mary and Marvin Keen – you remember them. One of the most bizarre features of my life since I left the studio is that nowadays I never see stars anymore. Isn't that ridiculous? Someone like me who worked with them, who practically lives in Hollywood? Somehow I never get to see the stars anymore. I just miss them. 'Oh he left five minutes ago, bub,' or 'Oh no, I think she's on location in Europe, she hasn't been here for weeks.' The same old story.

I think that's what Jayette's referring to when she asks if I've lucked-out. She knows I'm still hanging in there, waiting. I mean, I've kept on my agent. The way I see it is that once you've been in front of the cameras something's going to keep driving you on until you get back. I know it'll happen to me again one day, I just have this feeling inside.

After breakfast I jog back up the beach to where I left the car. One morning I got to thinking about Jayette. What does she think when she sees me now and remembers me from the days of 'The Scrantons'? It seems to me that everybody in their life is at least two people. Once when you're a child and once when you're an adult. It's the saddest thing. I don't just mean that you see things differently when you're a child – that's something else again – what's sad is that you can't seem to keep the personality. I know I'm not the same person anymore as young Chuck Scranton was, and I find that depressing. I could meet little Charlie on the beach today and say 'Look, there goes a sharp kid.' And never recognize him, if you see what I mean. It's a shame.

I don't like the jog back so much, as all the people are coming out. Lying around, surfing, cruising, scoring, shooting up, tricking. Hell, the things I've seen on that sand, I could tell you a few stories. Sometimes I like to go down to El Segundo or Redondo beach just to feel normal.

I usually park the car on Santa Monica Palisades. I tidy up, change into my clothes and shave. I have a small battery-powered electric razor that I use. Then I have a beer, wander around, buy a newspaper. Mostly I then drive north to Malibu. There's a place I know where you can get a fair view of a longish stretch of the beach. It's almost impossible to get down there in summer; they don't like strangers. So I pull off the highway and climb this small dune-hill. I have a pair of opera glasses of my aunt's that I use to see better – my eyesight's not too hot. I spotted Rod Steiger one day, and Jane Fonda I think but I can't be sure, the glasses tend to fuzz everything a bit over four hundred yards. Anyway I like the quiet on that dune, it's restful.

I have been down on to Malibu beach, but only in the winter season. The houses are all shut up but you can still get the feel of it. Some people were having a bar-b-q one day. It looked good. They had a fire going on a big porch that jutted out over the sand. They waved and shouted when I went past.

Lunch is bad. The worst part of the day for me because I have to go home. I live with my aunt. I call her my aunt though I'm not related to her at all. She was my mother's companion – I believe that's the right word – until my mother stuffed her face with a gross of Seconal one afternoon in a motel at Corona del Mar. I was fifteen then and Vanessa – my 'aunt' – became some kind of legal guardian to me and had control of all the money I'd made from 'The Scrantons'. Well, she bought an apartment in Beverly Glen because she liked the address. Man, was she swallowed by the realtor. They build these tiny apartment blocks on cliff-faces up the asshole of the big-name canyons just so you can say you live off Mulholland Drive or in Bel Air. It's a load. I'd rather live in Watts or on Imperial highway. I practically have to rope-up and wear crampons to get to my front door. And it is mine. I paid for it.

Maybe that's why Vanessa never leaves her bed. It's just too much effort getting in and out of the house. She just stays in bed all day and eats, watches TV and feeds her two dogs. I only go in there for lunch; it's my only 'family' ritual. I take a glass of milk and a salad sandwich but she phones out for pizza and enchiladas and burgers – any kind of crap she can smear over her face and down her front. She's really grown fat in the ten years since my mother bombed out. But she still sits up in bed with those hairy yipping dogs under her armpits, and she's got her top and bottom false eyelashes, her hairpiece and purple lipstick on. I say nothing usually. For someone who never gets out she sure can talk a lot. She wears these tacky satin and lace peignoirs, shows half her chest. Her breasts look like a couple of Indian clubs rolling around under the shimmer. It's unfair I suppose, but when I drive back into the foothills I like to think I'm going to have a luncheon date with . . . someone like Grace Kelly – as was – or maybe Alexis Smith. I don't know. I wouldn't mind a meal and a civilized conversation with some nice people like that. But lunch with Vanessa? Thanks for nothing, pal. God, you can keep it. She's a real klutz. I'm sure Grace and Alexis would never let themselves get that way – you know, like Vanessa's always dropping tacos down her cleavage or smearing mustard on her chins.

I always get depressed after lunch. It figures, I hear you say. I go to my room and sometimes I have a drink (I don't smoke, so dope's out). Other days I play my guitar or else work on my screenplay. It's called 'Walk. Don't Walk.' I get a lot of good ideas after lunch for some reason. That's when I got the idea for my screenplay. It just came to me. I remembered how I'd been stuck one day at the corner of Arteria boulevard and Normandie avenue. There was a pile of traffic and the pedestrian signs were going berserk. 'Walk' would come on so I'd start across. Two seconds later 'Don't Walk' so I go back. Then on comes 'Walk' again. This went on for ten minutes: 'Walk. Don't Walk. Walk. Don't Walk.' I was practically out of my box. But what really stunned me was the way I just stayed there and obeyed the goddam machine for so long – I never even thought about going it alone. Then one afternoon after lunch it came to me that it was a neat image for life; just the right kind of metaphor for the whole can of worms. The final scene of this movie is going to be a slow crane shot away from this malfunctioning traffic sign going 'Walk. Don't Walk.' Then the camera pulls further up and away in a helicopter and you see that in fact the whole city is fouled up because of this one sign flashing. They don't know what to do; the programming's gone wrong. It's a great final scene. Only problem is I'm having some difficulty writing my way towards it. Still, it'll come, I guess.

In the late afternoon I go to work. I work at the Beverly Hills Hotel. Vanessa's brother-in-law got me the job. I park cars. I keep hoping I'm going to park the car of someone really important. Frank – that's Vanessa's brother-in-law – will say to me 'Give this one a shine up, Charlie, it belongs to so and so, he produced this film,' or 'That guy's the money behind X's new movie,' or 'Look out, he's Senior Vice President of Something incorporated.' I say big deal. These guys hand me the keys – they all look like bank clerks. If that's the movies nowadays I'm not sure I want back in.

Afternoons are quiet at the hotel so I catch up on my reading. I'm reading Camus at the moment but I think I've learnt all I can from him so I'm going on to Jung. I don't know too much about Jung but I'm told he was really into astrology which has always been a pet interest of mine. One thing I will say for quitting the movies when I did means that I didn't miss out on my education. I hear that some of these stars today are really dumb; you know, they've got their brains in their neck and points south.

After work I drive back down to the Santa Monica pier and think about what I'm going to do all night. The Santa Monica pier is a kind of special place for me: it's the last place I saw my wife and son. I got married at seventeen and was divorced by twenty-two, though we were apart for a couple of years before that. Her name was Harriet. It was okay for a while but I don't think she liked Vanessa. Anyway, get this. She left me for a guy who was the assistant manager in the credit collection department of a large mail order firm. I couldn't believe it when she told me. I said to her when she moved out that it had to be the world's most boring job and did she know what she was getting into? I mean, what sort of person do you have to be to take on that kind of work? The bad thing was she took my son Skiff with her. It's a dumb name I know, but at the time he was born all the kids were being called things like Sky and Saffron and Powie, and I was really sold on sailing. I hope he doesn't hold it against me.

The divorce was messy and she got custody, though I'll never understand why. She had left some clothes at the house and wanted them back so she suggested we meet at the end of the Santa Monica pier for some reason. I didn't mind, it was the impetuous side to her nature that first attracted me. I handed the clothes over. She was a bit tense. Skiff was running about; he didn't seem to know who I was. She was smoking a lot; those long thin menthol cigarettes. I really didn't say anything much at all, asked her how she was, what school Skiff was going to. Then she just burst out 'Take a good look, Charlie, then don't come near us ever again!' Her exact words. Then they went away.

So I go down to the end of the pier most nights and look out at the ocean and count the planes going in to land at L.A. International and try to work things out. Just the other evening I wandered up the beach a way and this thin-faced man with short grey hair came up to me and said 'Jordan, is that you?' And when he saw he'd made a mistake he smiled a nice smile, apologized and walked off. It was only this morning that I thought it might have been Christopher Isherwood himself. The more I think about it the more convinced I become. What a perfect opportunity and I had to go and miss it. As I say: 'Walk. Don't Walk.' That's the bottom line.

I suppose I must have been preoccupied. The pier brings back all these memories like some private video-loop, and my head gets to feel like it's full of birds all flapping around trying to get out. And also things haven't been so good lately. On Friday Frank told me not to bother showing up at the hotel next week, I can't seem to make any headway with the screenplay and for the last three nights Vanessa's tried to climb into my bed.

Well, tonight I think I'll drive to this small bar I know on Sunset. Nothing too great, a little dark. They do a nice white wine with peach slices in it, and there's some topless, some go-go, and I hear tell that Bobby de Niro sometimes shows up for a drink.

William Boyd

■ YOU SHOULD HAVE SEEN THE MESS ■

I am now more than glad that I did not pass into the grammar school five years ago, although it was a disappointment at the time. I was always good at English, but not so good at the other subjects!!

I am glad that I went to the secondary modern school, because it was only constructed the year before. Therefore, it was much more hygienic than the grammar school. The secondary modern was light and airy, and the walls were painted with a bright washable gloss. One day, I was sent over to the grammar school, with a note for one of the teachers, and you should have seen the mess! The corridors were dusty, and I saw dust on the window ledges, which were chipped. I saw into one of the classrooms. It was very untidy in there.

I am also glad that I did not go to the grammar school, because of what it does to one's habits. This may appear to be a strange remark, at first sight. It is a good thing to have an education behind you, and I do not believe in ignorance, but I have had certain experiences, with educated people, since going out into the world.

I am seventeen years of age, and left school two years ago last month. I had my A certificate for typing, so got my first job as a junior, in a solicitor's office. Mum was pleased at this, and Dad said it was a first-class start, as it was an old-established firm. I must say that when I went for the interview, I was surprised at the windows, and the stairs up to the offices were also far from clean. There was a little waiting room, where some of the elements were missing from the gas fire, and the carpet on the floor was worn. However, Mr. Heygate's office, into which I was shown for the interview, was better. The furniture was old, but it was polished, and there was a good carpet, I will say that. The glass of the bookcase was very clean.

I was to start on the Monday, so along I went. They took me to the general office, where there were two senior shorthand-typists, and a clerk, Mr. Gresham, who was far from smart in appearance. You should have seen the mess!! There was no floor covering whatsoever, and so dusty everywhere. There were shelves all round the room, with old box files on them. The box files were falling to pieces, and all the old papers inside them were crumpled. The worst shock of all was the tea-cups. It was my duty to make tea, mornings and afternoons. Miss Bewlay showed me where everything was kept. It was kept in an old orange box, and the cups were all cracked. There were not enough saucers to go round, etc. I will not go into the facilities, but they were also far from hygienic. After three days, I told Mum, and she was upset, most of all about the cracked cups. We never keep a cracked cup, but throw it out, because those cracks can harbour germs. So Mum gave me my own cup to take to the office.

Then at the end of the week, when I got my salary, Mr. Heygate said, 'Well, Lorna, what are you going to do with your first pay?' I did not like him saying this, and I nearly passed a comment, but I said, 'I don't know.' He said, 'What do you do in the evenings, Lorna? Do you watch Telly?' I did take this as an insult, because we call it TV, and his remark made me out to be uneducated. I just stood, and did not answer, and he looked surprised. Next day, Saturday, I told Mum and Dad about the facilities, and we decided I should not go back to that job. Also, the desks in the general office were rickety. Dad was indignant, because Mr. Heygate's concern was flourishing, and he had letters after his name.

Everyone admires our flat, because Mum keeps it spotless, and Dad keeps doing things to it. He has done it up all over, and got permission from the Council to re-modernize the kitchen. I well recall the Health Visitor remarking to Mum, 'You could eat off your floor, Mrs. Merrifield.' It is true that you could eat your lunch off Mum's floors, and any hour of the day or night you will find every corner spick and span.

Next, I was sent by the agency to a publisher's for an interview, because of being good at English. One look was enough!! My next interview was a success, and I am still at Low's Chemical Co. It is a modern block, with a quarter of an hour rest period, morning and afternoon. Mr. Marwood is very smart in appearance. He is well spoken, although he has not got a university education behind him. There is special lighting over the desks, and the typewriters are the latest models.

So I am happy at Low's. But I have met other people, of an educated type, in the past year, and it has opened my eyes. It so happened that I had to go to the doctor's house, to fetch a prescription for my young brother, Trevor, when the epidemic was on. I rang the bell, and Mrs. Darby came to the door. She was small, with fair hair, but too long, and a green maternity dress. But she was very nice to me. I had to wait in their living-room, and you should have seen the state it was in! There were broken toys on the carpet, and the ash trays were full up. There were contemporary pictures on the walls, but the furniture was not contemporary, but old-fashioned, with covers which were past standing up to another wash, I should say. To cut a long story short, Dr. Darby and Mrs. Darby have always been very kind to me, and they meant everything for the best. Dr. Darby is also short and fair, and they have three children, a girl and a boy, and now a baby boy.

When I went that day for the prescription, Dr. Darby said to me, 'You look pale, Lorna. It's the London atmosphere. Come on a picnic with us, in the car, on Saturday.' After that I went with the Darbys more and more. I liked them, but I did not like the mess, and it was a surprise. But I also kept in with them for the opportunity of meeting people, and Mum and Dad were pleased that I had made nice friends. So I did not say anything about the cracked lino, and the paintwork all chipped. The children's clothes were very shabby for a doctor, and she changed them out of their school clothes when they came home from school, into those worn out garments. Mum always kept us spotless to go out to play, and I do not like to say it, but those Darby children frequently looked like the Leary family, which the Council evicted from our block, as they were far from houseproud.

One day, when I was there, Mavis (as I called Mrs. Darby by then) put her head out of the window, and shouted to the boy, 'John, stop peeing over the cabbages at once. Pee on the lawn.' I did not know which way to look. Mum would never say a word like that from the window, and I know for a fact that Trevor would never pass water outside, not even bathing in the sea.

I went there usually at the week-ends, but sometimes on week-days, after supper. They had an idea to make a match for me with a chemist's assistant, whom they had taken up too. He was an orphan, and I do not say there was anything wrong with that. But he was not accustomed to those little extras that I was. He was a good looking boy, I will say that. So I went once to a dance, and twice to films with him. To look at, he was quite clean in appearance. But there was only hot water at the week-end at his place, and he said that a bath once a week was sufficient. Jim (as I called Dr. Darby by then) said it was sufficient also, and surprised me. He did not have much money, and I do not hold that against him. But there was no hurry for me, and I could wait for a man in a better position, so that I would not miss those little extras. So he started going out with a girl from the coffee bar, and did not come to the Darbys very much then.

There were plenty of boys at the office, but I will say this for the Darbys, they had lots of friends coming and going, and they had interesting conversation, although sometimes it gave me a surprise, and I did not know where to look. And sometimes they had people who were very down and out, although there is no need to be. But most of the guests were different, so it made a comparison with the boys at the office, who were not so educated in their conversation.

Now it was near the time for Mavis to have her baby, and I was to come in at the week-end, to keep an eye on the children, while the help had her day off. Mavis did not go away to have her baby, but would have it at home, in their double bed, as they did not have twin beds, although he was a doctor. A girl I knew, in our block, was engaged, but was let down, and even she had her baby in the labour ward. I was sure a bedroom was not hygienic for having a baby, but I did not mention it.

One day, after the baby boy came along, they took me in the car to the country, to see Jim's mother. The baby was put in a carry-cot at the back of the car. He began to cry, and without a word of a lie, Jim said to him over his shoulder, 'Oh shut your gob, you little bastard.' I did not know what to do, and Mavis was smoking a cigarette. Dad would not dream of saying such a thing to Trevor or I. When I arrived at Jim's mother's place, Jim said, 'It's a fourteenth-century cottage, Lorna.'

I could well believe it. It was very cracked and old, and it made one wonder how Jim could let his old mother live in this tumble-down cottage, as he was so good to everyone else. So Mavis knocked at the door, and the old lady came. There was not much anyone could do to the inside. Mavis said, 'Isn't it charming, Lorna?' If that was a joke, it was going too far. I said to the old Mrs. Darby, 'Are you going to be re-housed?' but she did not understand this, and I explained how you have to apply to the Council, and keep at them. But it was funny that the Council had not done something already, when they go round condemning. Then old Mrs. Darby said, 'My dear, I shall be re-housed in the Grave.' I did not know where to look.

There was a carpet on the wall, which I think was there to hide a damp spot. She had a good TV set, I will say that. But some of the walls were bare brick, and the facilities were outside, through the garden. The furniture was far from new.

One Saturday afternoon, as I happened to go to the Darbys, they were just going off to a film and they took me too. It was the Curzon, and afterwards we went to a flat in Curzon Street. It was a very clean block, I will say that, and there were good carpets at the entrance. The couple there had contemporary furniture, and they also spoke about music. It was a nice place, but there was no Welfare Centre to the flats, where people could go for social intercourse, advice, and guidance. But they were well spoken, and I met Willy Morley, who was an artist. Willy sat beside me, and we had a drink. He was young, dark, with a dark shirt, so one could not see right away if he was clean. Soon after this, Jim said to me, 'Willy wants to paint you, Lorna. But you'd better ask your Mum.' Mum said it was all right if he was a friend of the Darbys.

I can honestly say that Willy's place was the most unhygienic place I have seen in my life. He said I had an unusual type of beauty, which he must capture. This was when we came back to his place from the restaurant. The light was very dim, but I could see the bed had not been made, and the sheets were far from clean. He said he must paint me, but I told Mavis I did not like to go back there. 'Don't you like Willy?' she asked. I could not deny that I liked Willy, in a way. There was something about him, I will say that. Mavis said, 'I hope he hasn't been making a pass at you, Lorna.' I said he had not done so, which was almost true, because he did not attempt to go to the full extent. It was always unhygienic when I went to Willy's place, and I told him so once, but he said, 'Lorna, you are a joy.' He had a nice way, and he took me out in his car, which was a good one, but dirty inside, like his place. Jim said one day, 'He has pots of money, Lorna,' and Mavis said, 'You might make a man of him, as he is keen on you.' They always said Willy came from a good family.

But I saw that one could not do anything with him. He would not change his shirt very often, or get clothes, but he went round like a tramp, lending people money, as I have seen with my own eyes. His place was in a terrible mess, with empty bottles, and laundry in the corner. He gave me several gifts over the period, which I took as he would have only given them away, but he never tried to go to the full extent. He never painted my portrait, as he was painting fruit on a table all that time, and they said his pictures were marvellous, and thought Willy and I were getting married.

One night, when I went home, I was upset as usual, after Willy's place. Mum and Dad had gone to bed, and I looked round our kitchen which is done in primrose and white. Then I went into the living room, where Dad has done one wall in a patterned paper, deep rose and white, and the other walls pale rose, with white woodwork. The suite is new, and Mum keeps everything beautiful. So it came to me, all of a sudden, what a fool I was, going with Willy. I agree to equality, but as to me marrying Willy, as I said to Mavis, when I recall his place, and the good carpet gone greasy, not to mention the paint oozing out of the tubes, I think it would break my heart to sink so low.

Muriel Spark

■ REQUEST STOP ■

A queue at a Request Bus Stop. A WOMAN *at the head, with a* SMALL MAN *in a raincoat next to her, two other* WOMEN *and a* MAN.

WOMAN [*to* SMALL MAN]:   I beg your pardon, what did you say?
    Pause.

    All I asked you was if I could get a bus from here to Shepherds Bush.

Pause.

    Nobody asked you to start making insinuations.

Pause.

    Who do you think you are?

Pause.

    Huh. I know your sort, I know your type. Don't worry, I know all about people like you.

Pause.

    We can all tell where you come from. They're putting your sort inside every day of the week.

Pause.

    All I've got to do, is report you, and you'd be standing in the dock in next to no time. One of my best friends is a plain clothes detective.

Pause.

I know all about it. Standing there as if butter wouldn't melt in your mouth. Meet you in a dark alley it'd be ... another story. [*To the others, who stare into space.*] You heard what this man said to me. All I asked him was if I could get a bus from here to Shepherds Bush. [*To him.*] I've got witnesses, don't you worry about that.

Pause.

Impertinence.

Pause.

Ask a man a civil question he treats you like a threepenny bit. [*To him.*] I've got better things to do, my lad, I can assure you. I'm not going to stand here and be insulted on a public highway. Anyone can tell you're a foreigner. I was born just around the corner. Anyone can tell you're just up from the country for a bit of a lark. I know your sort.

Pause.

She goes to a LADY.

Excuse me lady. I'm thinking of taking this man up to the magistrate's court, you heard him make that crack, would you like to be a witness?

The LADY *steps into the road.*

LADY: Taxi...

She disappears.

WOMAN: We know what sort she is. [*Back to position.*] I was the first in this queue.

Pause.

Born just round the corner. Born and bred. These people from the country haven't the faintest idea of how to behave. Peruvians. You're bloody lucky I don't put you on a charge. You ask a straightforward question –

The others suddenly thrust out their arms at a passing bus. They run off left after it. The WOMAN, *alone, clicks her teeth and mutters. A man walks from the right to the stop, and waits. She looks at him out of the corner of her eye. At length she speaks shyly, hesitantly, with a slight smile.*

Excuse me. Do you know if I can get a bus from here ... to Marble Arch?

Harold Pinter

■ Last to Go ■

A coffee stall. A BARMAN *and an old* NEWSPAPER SELLER. *The* BARMAN *leans on his counter, the* OLD MAN *stands with tea. Silence.*

MAN: You was a bit busier earlier.
BARMAN: Ah.
MAN: Round about ten.
BARMAN: Ten, was it?
MAN: About then.

> *Pause.*

> I passed by here about then.
BARMAN: Oh yes?
MAN: I noticed you were doing a bit of trade.

> *Pause.*

BARMAN: Yes, trade was very brisk here about ten.
MAN: Yes, I noticed.

> *Pause.*

> I sold my last one about then. Yes. About nine forty-five.
BARMAN: Sold your last then, did you?
MAN: Yes, my last 'Evening News' it was. Went about twenty to ten.

> *Pause.*

BARMAN: 'Evening News', was it?
MAN: Yes.

> *Pause.*

> Sometimes it's the 'Star' is the last to go.
BARMAN: Ah.
MAN: Or the . . . whatsisname.
BARMAN: 'Standard'.
MAN: Yes.

> *Pause.*

> All I had left tonight was the 'Evening News'.

> *Pause.*

BARMAN: Then that went, did it?
MAN: Yes.

> *Pause.*

      Like a shot.

Pause.

BARMAN: You didn't have any left, eh?
MAN: No. Not after I sold that one.

Pause.

BARMAN: It was after that you must have come by here then, was it?
MAN: Yes, I come by here after that, see, after I packed up.
BARMAN: You didn't stop here though, did you?
MAN: When?
BARMAN: I mean, you didn't stop here and have a cup of tea then, did you?
MAN: What, about ten?
BARMAN: Yes.
MAN: No, I went up to Victoria.
BARMAN: No, I thought I didn't see you.
MAN: I had to go up to Victoria.

Pause.

BARMAN: Yes, trade was very brisk here about then.

Pause.

MAN: I went to see if I could get hold of George.
BARMAN: Who?
MAN: George.

Pause.

BARMAN: George who?
MAN: George . . . whatsisname.
BARMAN: Oh.

Pause.

      Did you get hold of him?
MAN: No. No, I couldn't get hold of him. I couldn't locate him.
BARMAN: He's not about much now, is he?

Pause.

MAN: When did you last see him then?
BARMAN: Oh, I haven't seen him for years.
MAN: No, nor me.

Pause.

BARMAN: Used to suffer very bad from arthritis.
MAN: Arthritis?

BARMAN: Yes.

MAN: He never suffered from arthritis.

BARMAN: Suffered very bad.

Pause.

MAN: Not when I knew him.

Pause.

BARMAN: I think he must have left the area.

Pause.

MAN: Yes, it was the 'Evening News' was the last to go tonight.

BARMAN: Not always the last though, is it, though?

MAN: No. Oh no. I mean sometimes it's the 'News'. Other times it's one of the others. No way of telling beforehand. Until you've got your last one left, of course. Then you can tell which one it's going to be.

BARMAN: Yes.

Pause.

MAN: Oh yes.

Pause.

I think he must have left the area.

Harold Pinter

■ COMPARISONS ■

I compare the room to a cell
and claim we've locked the world out.
You point out it's that kind of hotel.
I say the collapsed window blind
resembles a defunct concertina.
You say it won't help us find
a cover for the naked window.
To me, the coathangers' jangle
(it sets your teeth on edge, I know)
is like a skeleton's laughter.
And isn't the sink, with its dangle
of chain, a bit of a godless altar?
You point to the drip, eye the stain
and conclude it won't hold water.
You tell me I'm full of unfeeling

(continued over...)

and unhelpful comparisons.
Very well: the cracks in the ceiling
remind me of no far horizons.
These rips in the sheets are nothing
like old men's toothless grins.
But now I need help with something:
how to look into the literal mirror,
nailed above the shelf-like shelf,
and find a way not to compare
that half-smiling, human error
to this cracked, but shining self.

Brian McCabe

■ SECRETS ■

He had been called to be there at the end. His Great Aunt Mary had been dying for some days now and the house was full of relatives. He had just left his girlfriend's home – they had been studying for 'A' levels together – and had come back to the house to find all the lights spilling onto the lawn and a sense of purpose which had been absent from the last few days.

He knelt at the bedroom door to join in the prayers. His knees were on the wooden threshold and he edged them forward onto the carpet. They had tried to wrap her fingers around a crucifix but they kept loosening. She lay low on the pillow and her face seemed to have shrunk by half since he had gone out earlier in the night. Her white hair was damped and pushed back from her forehead. She twisted her head from side to side, her eyes closed. The prayers chorused on, trying to cover the sound she was making deep in her throat. Someone said about her teeth and his mother leaned over her and said, 'That's the pet', and took her dentures from her mouth. The lower half of her face seemed to collapse. She half opened her eyes but could not raise her eyelids enough and showed only crescents of white.

'Hail Mary full of grace . . .' the prayers went on. He closed his hands over his face so that he would not have to look but smelt the trace of his girlfriend's handcream from his hands. The noise, deep and guttural, that his aunt was making became intolerable to him. It was as if she were drowning. She had lost all the dignity he knew her to have. He got up from the floor and stepped between the others who were kneeling and went into her sitting-room off the same landing.

He was trembling with anger or sorrow, he didn't know which. He sat in the brightness of her big sitting-room at the oval table and waited for something to happen. On the table was a cut-glass vase of irises, dying because she had been in bed for over a week. He sat staring at them. They were withering from the tips

98

inward, scrolling themselves delicately, brown and neat. Clearing up after themselves. He stared at them for a long time until he heard the sounds of women weeping from the next room.

■ ■ ■ ■ ■

His aunt had been small – her head on a level with his when she sat at her table – and she seemed to get smaller each year. Her skin fresh, her hair white and waved and always well washed. She wore no jewelry except a cameo ring on the third finger of her right hand and, around her neck, a gold locket on a chain. The white classical profile on the ring was almost worn through and had become translucent and indistinct. The boy had noticed the ring when she had read to him as a child. In the beginning fairy tales, then as he got older extracts from famous novels, *Lorna Doone*, *Persuasion*, *Wuthering Heights* and her favourite extract, because she read it so often, Pip's meeting with Miss Havisham from *Great Expectations*. She would sit with him on her knee, her arms around him and holding the page flat with her hand. When he was bored he would interrupt her and ask about the ring. He loved hearing her tell of how her grandmother had given it to her as a brooch and she had had a ring made from it. He would try to count back to see how old it was. Had her grandmother got it from *her* grandmother? And if so what had she turned it into? She would nod her head from side to side and say, 'How would I know a thing like that?' keeping her place in the closed book with her finger.

'Don't be so inquisitive,' she'd say. 'Let's see what happens next in the story.'

One day she was sitting copying figures into a long narrow book with a dip pen when he came into her room. She didn't look up but when he asked her a question she just said, 'Mm?' and went on writing. The vase of irises on the oval table vibrated slightly as she wrote.

'What is it?' She wiped the nib on blotting paper and looked up at him over her reading glasses.

'I've started collecting stamps and Mama says you might have some.'

'Does she now – ?'

She got up from the table and went to the tall walnut bureau-bookcase standing in the alcove. From a shelf of the bookcase she took a small wallet of keys and selected one for the lock. There was a harsh metal shearing sound as she pulled the desk flap down. The writing area was covered with green leather which had dog-eared at the corners. The inner part was divided into pigeon holes, all bulging with papers. Some of them, envelopes, were gathered in batches nipped at the waist with elastic bands. There were postcards and bills and cashbooks. She pointed to the postcards.

'You may have the stamps on those,' she said. 'But don't tear them. Steam them off.'

She went back to the oval table and continued writing. He sat on the arm of the chair looking through the picture postcards – torchlight processions at Lourdes, brown photographs of town centres, dull black and whites of beaches backed by faded hotels. Then he turned them over and began to sort the stamps. Spanish, with a bald man, French with a rooster, German with funny jerky print, some Italian with what looked like a chimney-sweep's bundle and a hatchet.

'These are great,' he said. 'I haven't got any of them.'

'Just be careful how you take them off.'

'Can I take them downstairs?'

'Is your mother there?'

'Yes.'

'Then perhaps it's best if you bring the kettle up here.'

He went down to the kitchen. His mother was in the morning room polishing silver. He took the kettle and the flex upstairs. Except for the dipping and scratching of his aunt's pen the room was silent. It was at the back of the house overlooking the orchard and the sound of traffic from the main road was distant and muted. A tiny rattle began as the kettle warmed up, then it bubbled and steam gushed quietly from its spout. The cards began to curl slightly in the jet of steam but she didn't seem to be watching. The stamps peeled moistly off and he put them in a saucer of water to flatten them.

'Who is Brother Benignus?' he asked. She seemed not to hear. He asked again and she looked over her glasses.

'He was a friend.'

His flourishing signature appeared again and again. Sometimes Bro Benignus, sometimes Benignus and once Iggy.

'Is he alive?'

'No, he's dead now. Watch the kettle doesn't run dry.'

When he had all the stamps off he put the postcards together and replaced them in the pigeon-hole. He reached over towards the letters but before his hand touched them his aunt's voice, harsh for once, warned.

'A-A-A,' she moved her pen from side to side. 'Do-not-touch,' she said and smiled. 'Anything else, yes! That section, no!' She resumed her writing.

The boy went through some other papers and found some photographs. One was of a beautiful girl. It was very old-fashioned but he could see that she was beautiful. The picture was a pale brown oval set on a white square of card. The edges of the oval were misty. The girl in the photograph was young and had dark, dark hair scraped severely back and tied like a knotted rope on the top of her head – high arched eyebrows, her nose straight and thin, her mouth slightly smiling, yet not smiling – the way a mouth is after smiling. Her eyes looked out at him dark and knowing and beautiful.

'Who is that?' he asked.

'Why? What do you think of her?'

'She's all right.'

'Do you think she is beautiful?' The boy nodded.

'That's me,' she said. The boy was glad he had pleased her in return for the stamps.

Other photographs were there, not posed ones like Aunt Mary's but Brownie snaps of laughing groups of girls in bucket hats like German helmets and coats to their ankles. They seemed tiny faces covered in clothes. There was a photograph of a young man smoking a cigarette, his hair combed one way by the wind against a background of sea.

'Who is that in the uniform?' the boy asked.

'He's a soldier,' she answered without looking up.

'Oh,' said the boy. 'But who is he?'

'He was a friend of mine before you were born,' she said. Then added, 'Do I smell something cooking? Take your stamps and off you go. That's the boy.'

The boy looked at the back of the picture of the man and saw in black spidery ink 'John, Aug '15 Ballintoye'.

'I thought maybe it was Brother Benignus,' he said. She looked at him not answering.

'Was your friend killed in the war?'

At first she said no, but then she changed her mind.

'Perhaps he was,' she said, then smiled. 'You are far too inquisitive. Put it to use and go and see what is for tea. Your mother will need the kettle.' She came over to the bureau and helped tidy the photographs away. Then she locked it and put the keys on the shelf.

'Will you bring me up my tray?'

The boy nodded and left.

■ ■ ■ ■ ■

It was a Sunday evening, bright and summery. He was doing his homework and his mother was sitting on the carpet in one of her periodic fits of tidying out the drawers of the mahogany sideboard. On one side of her was a heap of paper scraps torn in quarters and bits of rubbish, on the other the useful items that had to be kept. The boy heard the bottom stair creak under Aunt Mary's light footstep. She knocked and put her head round the door and said that she was walking to Devotions. She was dressed in her good coat and hat and was just easing her fingers into her second glove. The boy saw her stop and pat her hair into place before the mirror in the hallway. His mother stretched over and slammed the door shut. It vibrated, then he heard the deeper sound of the outside door closing and her first few steps on the gravelled driveway. He sat for a long time wondering if he would have time or not. Devotions could take anything from twenty minutes to three quarters of an hour, depending on who was saying it.

Ten minutes must have passed, then the boy left his homework and went upstairs and into his aunt's sitting room. He stood in front of the bureau wondering, then he reached for the keys. He tried several before he got the right one. The desk flap screeched as he pulled it down. He pretended to look at the postcards again in case there were any stamps he had missed. Then he put them away and reached for the bundle of letters. The elastic band was thick and old, brittle almost, and when he took it off its track remained on the wad of letters. He carefully opened one and took out the letter and unfolded it, frail, khaki-coloured.

My dearest Mary, it began. I am so tired I can hardly write to you. I have spent what seems like all day censoring letters (there is a howitzer about 100 yds away firing every 2 minutes). The letters are heart-rending in their attempt to express what they cannot. Some of the men are illiterate, others almost so. I know that they feel as much as we do, yet they do not have the words to express it. That is your job in the schoolroom to give us generations who can read and write well. They have . . .

The boy's eye skipped down the page and over the next. He read the last paragraph.

Mary I love you as much as ever – more so that we cannot be together. I do not know which is worse, the hurt of this war or being separated from you. Give all my love to Brendan and all at home.

It was signed, scribbled with what he took to be John. He folded the paper carefully into its original creases and put it in the envelope. He opened another.

My love, it is thinking of you that keeps me sane. When I get a moment I open my memories of you as if I were reading. Your long dark hair – I always imagine you wearing the blouse with the tiny roses, the white one that opened down the back – your eyes that said so much without words, the way you lowered your head when I said anything that embarrassed you, and the clean nape of your neck.

The day I think about most was the day we climbed the head at Ballycastle. In a hollow, out of the wind, the air full of pollen and the sound of insects, the grass warm and dry and you lying beside me your hair undone, between me and the sun. You remember that that was where I first kissed you and the look of disbelief in your eyes that made me laugh afterwards.

It makes me laugh now to see myself savouring these memories standing alone up to my thighs in muck. It is everywhere, two, three feet deep. To walk ten yards leaves you quite breathless.

I haven't time to write more today so I leave you with my feet in the clay and my head in the clouds. I love you, John.

He did not bother to put the letter back into the envelope but opened another.

My dearest, I am so cold that I find it difficult to keep my hand steady enough to write. You remember when we swam the last two fingers of your hand went the colour and texture of candles with the cold. Well that is how I am all over. It is almost four days since I had any real sensation in my feet or legs. Everything is frozen. The ground is like steel.

Forgive me telling you this but I feel I have to say it to someone. The worst thing is the dead. They sit or lie frozen in the position they died. You can distinguish them from the living because their faces are the colour of slate. God help us when the thaw comes . . . This war is beginning to have an effect on me. I have lost all sense of feeling. The only emotion I have experienced lately is one of anger. Sheer white trembling anger. I have no pity or sorrow for the dead and injured. I thank God it is not me but I am enraged that it had to be them. If I live through this experience I will be a different person.

The only thing that remains constant is my love for you.

Today a man died beside me. A piece of shrapnel had pierced his neck as we were moving under fire. I pulled him into a crater and stayed with him until he died. I watched him choke and then drown in his blood.

I am full of anger which has no direction.

He sorted through the pile and read half of some, all of others. The sun had fallen low in the sky and shone directly into the room onto the pages he was reading, making the paper glare. He selected a letter from the back of the pile and shaded it with his hand as he read.

Dearest Mary, I am writing this to you from my hospital bed. I hope that you were not too worried about not hearing from me. I have been here, so they tell me, for two weeks and it took another two weeks before I could bring myself to write this letter.

I have been thinking a lot as I lie here about the war and about myself and about you. I do not know how to say this but I feel deeply that I must do something, must sacrifice something to make up for the horror of the past year. In some strange way Christ has spoken to me through the carnage . . .

Suddenly the boy heard the creak of the stair and he frantically tried to slip the letter back into its envelope but it crumpled and would not fit. He bundled them all together. He could hear his aunt's familiar puffing on the short stairs to her room. He spread the elastic band wide with his fingers. It snapped and the letters scattered. He pushed them into their pigeon hole and quickly closed the desk flap. The brass screeched loudly and clicked shut. At that moment his aunt came into the room.

'What are you doing boy?' she snapped.

'Nothing.' He stood with the keys in his hand. She walked to the bureau and opened it. The letters sprung out in an untidy heap.

'You have been reading my letters,' she said quietly. Her mouth was tight with the words and her eyes blazed. The boy could say nothing. She struck him across the side of the face.

'Get out,' she said. 'Get out of my room.'

The boy, the side of his face stinging and red, put the keys on the table on his way out. When he reached the door she called to him. He stopped, his hand on the handle.

'You are dirt,' she hissed, 'and always will be dirt. I shall remember this till the day I die.'

■ ■ ■ ■ ■

Even though it was a warm evening there was a fire in the large fireplace. His mother had asked him to light it so that she could clear out Aunt Mary's stuff. The room could then be his study, she said. She came in and seeing him at the table said, 'I hope I'm not disturbing you.'

'No.'

She took the keys from her pocket, opened the bureau and began burning papers and cards. She glanced quickly at each one before she flicked it onto the fire.

'Who was Brother Benignus?' he asked.

His mother stopped sorting and said, 'I don't know. Your aunt kept herself very much to herself. She got books from him through the post occasionally. That much I do know.'

She went on burning the cards. They built into strata, glowing red and black. Now and again she broke up the pile with the poker, sending showers of sparks up the chimney. He saw her come to the letters. She took off the elastic band and put it to one side with the useful things and began dealing the envelopes into the fire. She opened one and read quickly through it, then threw it on top of the burning pile.

'Mama,' he said.

'Yes?'

'Did Aunt Mary say anything about me?'

'What do you mean?'

'Before she died – did she say anything?'

'Not that I know of – the poor thing was too far gone to speak, God rest her.' She went on burning, lifting the corners of the letters with the poker to let the flames underneath them.

When he felt a hardness in his throat he put his head down on his books. Tears came into his eyes for the first time since she had died and he cried silently into the crook of his arm for the woman who had been his maiden aunt, his teller of tales, that she might forgive him.

Bernard MacLaverty

■ It's a Democracy, Isn't It? ■

I was standing on the corner of Lexington Avenue on a Sunday in May waiting for a bus. It was a gorgeous day, hot and golden, and there were not many people around. Sunday is more than a bearable day in New York because for one thing there are about a million less cars than usual. No trucks. Suburbanites in for the day pointing up and down and walking with their feet out. A couple of cabs parked outside a lunch-room, the drivers gone for a beer. A family or two hand in hand, taking the children off to the park. A well-dressed upper-crust couple coming across from Park Avenue also hand in hand – a very common sight in New York, for Americans are not much concerned in such matters with what looks proper or what the neighbours will think. A good day – the sort of day when, for all the panicky newspaper headlines, your faith in people, and their needs and inclinations, is restored.

Suddenly, I heard a ghost. It was a familiar ghost, an invisible man somewhere in mid-air saying in a brisk monotone – 'Strike. The count is two and two. Runners on first and third.' This lingo, or the language of which this is a snatch, is something you would hear in a hundred places – homes, cafés, saloons, cars – from then till the end of the first week in October. It is a radio sports announcer covering a ball game – a ball game being, as you probably know, a baseball game.

The voice was coming from nowhere. A young Negro couple, arm in arm, was ambling towards me. But the man's free arm carried a little box. Of course, it was a portable radio. They went down the subway steps, and as they pattered down into the darkness the voice went on floating up, more excited now: 'A base hit to left field. Fuselli's in, Rodgers coming into third.' Nobody else on the street seemed to notice or to care. But if you had cared, and wanted for one day to get away from radio, I don't know where you could have gone. Out at Coney Island, thousands of bodies would be lying in close proximity not only to thousands of other bodies but to hundreds of other little boxes, tuned high. And the air would be so full of 'He's out' and 'The bases are loaded' and 'Full count', that you'd have had quite a time knowing what the wild waves were saying.

This little picture is meant to produce a shudder in you. If it doesn't, then Britons are not what they used to be, and their passion for privacy, and what's more for respecting the next man's privacy, is dead and gone. Don't misunderstand me. I approve myself very strongly of this feeling. I share it. But it makes me all the less of an American. Only a week ago, I heard a plonking sound, allied to music, quite faint, coming up through the living-room floor. It was a neighbour in our apartment house who is either six years of age and a promising pianist or forty years of age and a dope . . . because she – why do I say 'she', I wonder? – has been stuck on that same piece for a month or two now. I grumbled about the sameness of her repertory, and my twelve-year-old daughter, idling over a book, said, 'Relax, Pop, you don't have to hear it if you don't want to.'

By this simple remark my daughter didn't mean that I could get up and go downstairs and start a riot, or that I could call the police or take out an injunction. She simply meant I should shut my mind to the sound. I made sure this is what she meant, because when I played aloud with the idea of strangling our tinkling neighbour, she said, 'I don't think that's very nice. She paid *her* rent too, you know.'

Now, I should like to say that I am proud of my daughter and usually turn to her for a response that is commonsensical and unshocked (by, so far as I can make out, anything in life). But I wasn't aware she had acquired so young a fundamental mood or attitude of what Americans call democracy. In Britain, one of the minor duties of good citizenship is not to disturb the private life of other citizens. In this country, it's the other way around – not to disturb other citizens who are enjoying their private life in public. That, as you see, is a heavily loaded interpretation of an attitude that is universal among Americans. And there are limits. Just the same, the decision of a Washington court of appeal not to let advertisers broadcast in public buses only shows how far you can go in America without being stopped.

Americans regard most of us born in Britain as dull, decent, amiable people but given to being rather testy about our rights. So 'Relax, Pop,' says my daughter and goes back to reading her book with one third of her mind, listening to the pianist downstairs with another lobe, and at the same time dreaming on all cylinders about some absent male of the species. Quite aside from the principle involved, this attitude entails a considerable physical feat. It is the ability not to hear what you don't want to hear, what the most famous radio critic in America calls 'selective deafness'. He says it is a faculty essential to an enjoyment of American radio, and it is a faculty that most visiting Britons would rather not develop. Because they soon learn, as Mr Crosby – John, not Bing – remarks, that the advertising people are aware of this conditioned reflex and so from year to year, like drug addicts, they increase the dose of the sales talk they cut into the programmes. Still, nobody hearing his favourite comedian or forum discussion or symphony concert bothers to turn off the 'plug'. He lets it chatter on about some soap that 'atomizes dirt' or a toothpaste that is 'kind to gums but murder on film'. And then, the ecstatic announcer stops, and so back to Bob Hope or 'Whither Europe?' or the second symphony of Beethoven.

To watch an American on a beach, or crowding into a subway, or buying a theatre ticket, or sitting at home with his radio on, tells you something about one aspect of the American character: the capacity to withstand a great deal of outside interference, so to speak; a willing acceptance of frenzy which, though it's never self-conscious, amounts to a willingness to let other people have and assert their own lively, and even offensive, character. They are a tough race in this. You are expected – far beyond what other peoples would say were the restraints of manners – to assume that one man's opinion is as good as another's. The expert is an American idol, but only in certain understood fields. He is safe from contradiction if his expertness is in a science – in medicine, technology, industrial research, or in making something with his hands (better, if he uses somebody else's hands, because that shows he has mastered a process which can be left to drones): such things as an automobile, a waterproof watch or a non-riding girdle. But when it comes to ideas about life and love and religion and education and architecture and painting and music, indeed all forms of pleasure, there is a national conviction that an expert is a phoney, or 'wants to be different', and that what matters is you should know what you like and – this is a democracy, isn't it? – speak up and say your piece. It may well be born from generations of living close to many races and many prejudices and temperaments and having to strike a liveable compromise that may not be as smooth as some other societies; but at least it is a society, a going concern, which had to be built not out of a theory but out of the urgent practical need to get along at all.

At any rate, if you want to live here in any spiritual comfort you have to allow for a wide variety of temperament in your friends and neighbours and approve a sharp clash of tastes. An insistence on privacy in such a society looks, as it would not look in Britain, like a form of conceit or neurosis, a refusal to admit the status quo by which you all live. So if the issue ever came up in argument, I think most Americans would say that it is merely elementary good manners and good citizenship to look on yourself as only one member of the community, whether that community is a town, a party, or a family.

It may be what makes Americans so easy-going about their children. I don't know if anyone has ever taken a statistical count, and there may be just as many nagging parents here as anywhere else, but my impression is that if you are what they used to call a severe disciplinarian with children, you get known to the neighbours as a crank. There is a sort of cheerful, unstated assumption that children will grow up and be polite soon enough and that there's no sense for the first fifteen years or so in pretending they are anything but inhabitants of the jungle. (There is a certain family pride in seeing your child become king or queen of the jungle.) The children themselves are of course not aware of being particularly bad or violent or ill-mannered. They have no other system to compare themselves with, and like all children don't even know that any other system exists. Remembering this, you can appreciate that if a six- or a ten- or a fifteen-year-old passes you on the street, looks up and says, 'Hi!' he is paying you far more the respect of genuine liking than if he said, 'Good morning, sir' – which would be a very alien, not to say sarcastic, sound in these parts.

The same sort of tolerance explains too, I think, such a seemingly irrelevant thing as the variety of men's clothes in a big city. There is not among Americans anything remotely resembling the uniform of the English city businessman. They dress for themselves, with their own tastes in ties, shirts, shoes; and this gives to an American street a colour, often a garishness, and it makes it pretty impossible for a foreigner to guess at the occupation of the other men around. With women, it is even more difficult. A flock of girls comes into a restaurant and you can't tell the débutante from the shop girl. I remember a Swedish girl on a ski-ing party watching the swirl of people in the snow and saying, 'Which are the nice people? Who are my kind? Give me a sign.' There are signs. But they are small and subtle and would take her years to learn. And if she stayed here long, she would insensibly shed the signs she sought.

I was taking an Englishman the other night up to my apartment, and as we approached the entrance of the apartment house, I saw a man who lives in the building polishing the radiator of his car. I hissed to call my friend's attention to him as we came close. 'Tell me quick,' I said, 'what sort of an American is this – I mean is he a banker, a real-estate agent, a baseball player or what? – look him over.' My friend leered politely at him sideways. He was a middle-aged dark man, with a black moustache and big eyes. He was hatless. He had on a blue sports coat, slacks of a different colour, a button-down collar and a bright tie. He was polishing away and coughing smoke all over the radiator. Then he bent down to start on the wheels. Standing genially over him was the janitor, saying the utterly meaningless sentence, as we came on it: 'No, sir, not for my money . . . but some guys are that crazy, I reckon.' When we got inside I looked at my friend.

'Oh, I don't know,' he said, 'I should say an advertising man or perhaps the owner of a chain of drugstores.'

'That,' I said, as we went into the lift, 'is a dethroned Archduke.'

He was dethroned by the bullet that shot his great-uncle and started the First World War.

Alistair Cooke

[Mr Cooke would like to point out that although this talk was broadcast almost fifty years ago, he believes it is just as true of America today.]

■ *EXTRACT FROM* LIFE ON EARTH ■

The bones of many of the smaller dinosaurs make it clear that they were able, at least on occasion, to move very swiftly. From that we can deduce that, at least at times, their blood temperature was quite high. It may be that many were able to generate heat within their bodies. To what extent they were able to maintain a temperature constant within a few degrees at all times is a question that is much debated. All contemporary endotherms are equipped with some kind of heat insulation above or just below their skins – hair, fat or feathers. Without it, the demands on their energy would be intolerable. No reptile skin has such insulation today; nor is there any evidence that the dinosaurs were better provided for.

Problems of body temperature may well have brought about the fall of the dinosaur dynasty. Their end is portrayed with graphic clarity in the rocks of the Montana badlands. Here, horizontal beds of sandstones and mudstones, that were laid down 60 to 70 million years ago, have been sliced and gouged by the melting snows of winter and the violent storms of summer into a wilderness of pinnacles, buttes and gullies. On the striped faces of the crumbling cliffs, trickles of brown fragments, like water stains from a dripping tap, show where fossil bones are weathering out. Among them are the remains of Triceratops, a huge horned dinosaur. In life, it grew to eight metres or so in length and a weight of nine tons. Its immense skull carried three horns, one above each eye and one on the tip of its nose, and a great bony frill that projected from the back of its head to protect the neck. It was a vegetarian, champing cycads that grew in the swamps. Its brain, one of the largest possessed by any dinosaur, weighed about a kilogram. It seems probable therefore that it was not only huge and powerful but, compared with other creatures alive at the time, relatively intelligent. But that did not save it.

Just above the level at which its most recent bones are found, a thin deposit of coal rules a black, precise line that can be traced in cliff after cliff across Montana and over the Canadian border into Alberta. It must represent a short-lived but widespread swamp forest, and it marks the death of the dinosaurs. Immediately below it you can find the remains not only of Triceratops, but of at least ten other species of dinosaur. Above it there are none.

There have been many suggestions as to what brought the dinosaurs to their end. The more extreme require some kind of global catastrophe. They can be disregarded because, after all, it was only the dinosaurs that disappeared, not the whole of animal life – or even all the reptiles. Another theory suggests that the mammals, which at this time were on the brink of their great expansion, began to compete with the dinosaur for food and, perhaps because of their superior intelligence, were so successful that the dinosaurs were displaced and exterminated. The Montana fossil beds show why this could not have been so. They contain not only gigantic bones but minute ones, bones so tiny that the naked eye has great difficulty in finding them unaided. Fortunately, a species of ant in the area comes to the fossil hunter's aid. It builds low smooth mounds over its nests which it roofs with carefully selected gravel chips of a particular size. If you search through them you find that some are not stone but tiny cone-shaped teeth. These belonged to a shrew-like creature only a few centimetres long, one of the very first of the mammals. Mammals had already been in existence for many millions of years, but no sign of any bigger species has been found living at the same time as the dinosaurs. It is just possible that such a small creature could have preyed on dinosaur eggs, but it seems extremely unlikely that it could have done so with such intensity that it exterminated a single species, let alone the entire dinosaur group. Nor is it credible that it robbed the dinosaurs of their food or in some way out-manoeuvred them with its greater intelligence.

The Montana badlands provide evidence of yet another but more convincing explanation. In beds a little way above the final black marker of coal, there are some excellently preserved fossilised tree stumps. Triceratops and other dinosaurs of the time had lived in forests of cycads and ferns. These stumps belonged to a very different tree. Sequoia, the coniferous redwood. Today, and almost certainly then, the redwood preferred a cool climate. Its presence here is only one element in a great body of evidence which shows that about 63 million years ago, coinciding very closely with the disappearance of the dinosaurs, the world went through a great change of climate. It got colder.

This may very well have killed the dinosaurs. While it is true that a big body retains its heat for a long time, it is also true that it takes a very long time to regain it once it has been lost. Even if some of the dinosaurs had the ability to generate heat internally to some degree, a succession of bitterly cold nights could have drained a big dinosaur of its heat beyond all recovery. With its body badly chilled, it might not be able to summon sufficient energy to move its huge bulk and browse. So a steady cooling of the climate and an increasing seasonality producing severe winters, as there are now in Montana, may well have led to the extermination of the large herbivores. With them would go the carnivores that hunted them and were therefore dependent upon them. The pterosaurs, huddled on their cliffs, would be even more severely affected. The ichthyosaurs and plesiosaurs did not figure in this crisis. Their line, for some reason, had died out many millions of years earlier.

There were two ways to escape the effects of this increasing cold which are both practised by various reptiles alive today. One is to find a crevice in rocks or to bury yourself so that you are beyond the reach of the worst frosts and then fall into a state of suspended animation and hibernate. But that was only possible if you were small. Apatosaurus or Tyrannosaurus had no chance of doing so. The other was to take to the water. Since water retains heat much longer than air, the effects of a sudden cold snap are much reduced and the consequences of a long cold season can be avoided by swimming on migration to warmer latitudes. This was a way open to big creatures. It is not without significance that the three main types of reptile that survive today from the period of the dinosaurs – the crocodiles, the lizards, and the tortoises and turtles – can take advantage of one or other of these expedients.

David Attenborough

Strong tonic for the anaemic body politic

What's the point of politics? In a world where the globalised economy rules; in a world where the old powers of nation-states to make war, restrict the movement of things and people and control trade are failing; in the world of News International and the bond market why bother to spend your time working for political parties? Or voting, come to that? Polls show huge levels of voter cynicism. The economic programmes of the main parties – across Europe and the Americas, not just here – are more similar than ever before.

Power has been sucked to corporations and markets which are far beyond the reach of the ballot box. Could it be that the old game, with its paraphernalia of rosettes, leaflets, MPs, ministerial Jaguars and the rest is simply out of time? In Scotland the question ought to have a special poignance. Here, voters have been accustomed to their relative lack of power for a lot longer than the bulk of English voters; the oddity of having a country with a minority voice in its own governance has accustomed Scots to the compromises and defeats that English voters are only starting to face from Brussels. For many people, and most Scottish politicians, this has meant that questions of political power and political control become resolved into the campaign for a Scottish parliament. When it comes to political reform, this has been the issue that engulfs all others, the great catch-all, final solution. First get your parliament, then everything will follow.

Yet if Westminster has less and less purchase on the big issues – on trade, on the price of money, on environmental treaties, on the global culture – then how strong could a Scottish parliament possibly be? A splash of historical perspective may help here. The great age of European national awakening could be roughly placed in the century stretching from the 1820s to the 1920s, from Greece, through Italy, Poland, Germany and then on to the former countries of the Austro-Hungarian empire, Turkey and Ireland. It was the age when political progress seemed an uncomplicated thing, involving the creation of constitutional liberties, flags, parliamentary assemblies and secure national territories. But it was also the age when the power of the nation-state climbed towards its zenith, when war and modern bureaucracies created truly powerful political systems based on representative democracy, taxation and a national myth.

Scotland, it hardly needs to be said, began to notice this century of nationalism only when it had almost finished. But the dream of devolutionists and Scottish nationalists today owes a lot to that century of the nations, whose heady atmosphere of liberation was revived in our own times by the collapse of the Soviet empire and the re-emergence of the Czech Republic, Slovakia, Poland, Hungary and the Baltic states.

So far so dandy. The question which shouts out from the global changes of the Nineties is, however: is it all too late? Are these countries, and Scotland too, involving themselves in national reawakening just at the moment when the power of markets, global and regional organisations, treaties and multinational companies has rendered most of the traditional business of national politics redundant? In Scottish terms, if the MPs at Westminster seem increasingly powerless and feeble figures, what price Archie Broon MSP, sitting in Edinburgh? It's a serious question and a difficult one, a question which isn't in the interests of today's politicians to talk about. Why should they go around broadcasting their own relative powerlessness? But if we are going to take politics seriously – and measured most ways, whether by party membership, voting or public service, fewer and fewer of us do – then it is a question we cannot avoid. After a year of struggling with it, I was forced back to the basics.

The market is not, and cannot be, enough. A market economy, and a successful country, requires deferred gratification, high levels of education, long-termism, public order. It requires some belief in the future – some sense that contracts will be honoured, both big human contracts and small paper ones. It requires rootedness, a nourishing culture, in which the lessons learned by the country can be passed down from one generation to the next.

The American ecologist and writer Wendell Berry put it well when he asked whether countries could afford "this exclusive rule of competition, this purely economic economy? The great fault of this approach to things is that it is so drastically reductive: it does not permit us to live and work as human beings, as the best of our inheritance defines us. Rats and roaches live by competition under the law of supply and demand; it is the privilege of human beings to live under the laws of justice and mercy." He must be right. Without these elementary human goods,

societies can manage the occasional economic spurt, the odd period of boom, caused by newly-opened trade routes or some new technology; but they cannot last long. If we want to survive in the global economy, and thrive there, we need to be confident about ourselves. For that, we need to be confident about our institutions and our social relations.

Which takes us inevitably and clearly back to politics. The next question, though, is whether it is any longer possible to have political structures which are strong enough to check, civilise and answer the power of the market.

There are, of course, the new generation of global institutions, the huge regional trade blocs, the UN agencies and the World Trade Organisation, taking their place alongside Nato, the World Bank and the International Monetary Fund. They are clearly necessary, and also at least vestigially political, in that they are connected to voters via the governments that sponsor and fund them. A major part of the SNP's programme is now tied to getting Scotland more say in our local bloc, the European Union. The trouble is that these are too far away – far further than Westminster is from the Moray Firth. They are too high-up to be seriously counted as democratic bodies.

A better, and odder, answer is that strong local, nearer, power can indeed provide the nourishing culture that all long-term societies need. Companies and the markets could not survive without effective politicians, offering deals about territory, access, licences and so on. The nearer these deals are to us, the voters, the more real power we will have. Environmental treaties are global; but nuclear dumping, or arguments over link roads, are certainly not. What is needed is not to abandon politics, but to reform it.

Our system is like this. A small number of us, the uncommitted voters in the swing constituencies (500,000 across the UK, according to party strategists) are targeted by mendacious manifestos, and, every five years or so, choose the MPs who will sit in the parliament which has ceded most of its key powers over to the executive and the state which, in turn, is considerably less powerful than it was. So we have a weak influence over a weak legislature which in turn has only some influence over a weak state. If that's a virile democracy, God help us all.

In any reform programme, a Scottish parliament remains essential partly because of its democratic importance at home, but also because of the knock-on effect it will have in shaking up Westminster and remodelling politics throughout the UK. The Conservative efforts to find a peace formula for Northern Ireland, involving discussions about the Union, devolution, referendums, power-sharing, proportional representation and a bill of rights, give us some indication of how one piece of rethinking throws up a wider agenda.

But a Scottish parliament which sat on its bottom and tried to ape Westminster would be a short-lived disaster, just another latter-day manifestation of a mock-nation state out of touch with the big global forces. If it's to work it needs to become a blatant agent of political reform, spreading power further down, experimenting, taking risks, changing the rules of politi-cal debate, using referendums, thinking local as well as national. As an idiot optimist, I still think it's entirely possible that the catalyst for reforming the whole of British democracy will be that old school on that old hill in that old town of Edinburgh.

Andrew Marr
10.9.95

The Riviera touch

British tourists who salivate at the mere mention of Provence often turn their noses up at the Côte d'Azur. It has lately started to be regarded as Paradise Lost: dismissed as the crime-infested, overpopulated, polluted playground of the rich. That's if you can manage to beat your way through the traffic jams to get there in the first place.

A pity because the reasons why the rich colonised it in the first place are still there to savour – beautiful panoramic coastlines stretching back even in summer to the snow-capped Alps, blessed by hot summers and mild winters plus a rare quality of light which attracted painters such as Matisse, Renoir, Monet and Picasso. Why should the rich have it all to themselves?

Sure, it's a bit more expensive than the rest of France, but good food is still cheaper than in Britain and the recession has forced lots of restaurants to lower the prices of their cheaper menus. You can still eat well and economically in the winding back-streets of the old part of Cannes and in the old quarter of Nice. If you walk among the avenue of restaurants in the market behind the Quai des États-Unis in Nice you are positively solicited by waiters offering bargain buys and discounts.

But you don't have to go to the ritzy fringe of the South of France to savour the inexhaustible delights of the *real* south of France. This part of Provence can be enjoyed in layers depending on your mood. If you like basking on busy beaches, then the narrow coastal strip from Cannes through Nice and Antibes to Menton is for you.

If you don't, then try May and June before the French school holidays begin. Or drive westward along the coast road from La Napoule and you will encounter dozens of small beaches and rocky inlets, especially through Theoule, Miramar and Le Trayas towards St-Raphaël. The corniche cuts its way through the tortuous red rocks of the Esterel towards Miramar. If you see a line of French cars parked by the side of the road, it almost certainly means there is an inlet down below (with steps) popular with the locals, and where you can bathe in relative peace.

Or else stop by one of the hotels such as the Tour de L'Esquillon (where part of Scott Fitzgerald's *Tender Is the Night* was filmed) to buy a day-pass to its secluded rocky beach with a light lunch included. Walk up the road opposite the hotel and you come to one of the entrances to the Massif de L'Esterel. You will be stunned by the almost monastic calm of a mountain range where you can wander along sign-posted tracks for hours sometimes without encountering another soul.

What you can't see even from there is the artistic layer of this part of Provence which boasts more than 100 art galleries, museums and cultural centres. For what it's worth, the number of McDonald's restaurants is catching up fast.

Behind Nice and the teeming resorts of the Côte d'Azur lie the pink-remembered hills of the Back Country (L'Arrière-Pays). As the land level rises you can almost hear the restaurant prices dropping.

The joy of France is to discover your own villages, monuments, markets and restaurants. Take any road from Grasse into the Back Country (like the winding road to Vence through Le Bar sur Loup and Tourrette sur Loup) and you will soon find your own favourite spots. Further west, a drive to (and around) the huge and devouring Grand Canyon du Verdon is an unforgettable experience.

The French find it difficult to forgive the British for enjoying their country more than they do. No one but the British, deprived of predictable weather, warm sea and omnipresent cuisine, can fully appreciate the *contrast* that such a holiday brings.

Who but the Brits can take such hedonistic pleasure in driving through vineyards, eating *al fresco* or strolling at midnight among the plane trees (somehow much more exotic than their London cousins) in the hot after-burn of a Provencal day with the cigales hissing their haunting descant in the background. This may not justify the burden of the weather we have to endure for the rest of the year at home. But at least we can claim to enjoy our excursions to the Continent more than practically anyone else.

Victor Keegan

Nice work if you can define it

THE HUNGRY Monk at Jevington is the kind of restaurant sophisticated English travellers in France 20 years ago used to bore on about for hours: a little village in the middle of nowhere – it is actually about two miles off the main road just outside Eastbourne; turn off at Polegate and drive carefully through Wannock and the romantically named Filching – not much more than a pub, the best food you've ever eaten, why can't anybody in England cook like that, and so on and so forth.

It would be nice to think that sophisticated French travellers would now make the same kind of ecstatic discoveries here – it is listed in Michelin – but the last sophisticated French person I talked to about English country food, the wife of a former ambassador, held up her hands, allowed a dreamy expression to come into her eyes, and said: "*Ah, le Petit Chef! C'était dé-li-cieux!*"

What is also extremely nice about The Hungry Monk is the discreet Englishness of the service. There are eight tables, and the night we went there three girls were on duty, one managing the bar and reception, two working in the restaurant, the food arrived immediately we wanted it and none of them at any stage gave us a cabaret turn about our specials tonight including baby venison hearts drizzled in a sour cream and oyster custard whose price does not appear on the menu.

There was a party of international tennis players at the other end of the room and anywhere else I would have been tempted to ask the waitress who they were: at The Hungry Monk such questions would seem intrusive.

Not that it is by any means posh: the entrance is through a heavy medievalised door on the lane, there are a lot of low beams and there is a variety of pictures on the walls, some of them humorous in tone and featuring monks. The tables are dark polished wood, the furnishings comfortable and unobtrusive. The only indicator of the restaurant's well established reputation is a heap of food guides for sale on a table by the door and their own cook books, priced at £3.50.

The set dinner menu, offering a choice of seven starters, nine main courses and puddings, cost £21.90 a head.

I started with seared scallops with samphire and fine bacon, which carried a supplement of £1.75, and my wife, who was in a combative mood, asked for toasted goat cheese and pistachio soufflé. There is a good wine list and we ordered a bottle of St Christoly, a Cru Bourgeois from the Médoc, which was excellent and very reasonable at £13.64.

What my wife for some reason wanted to discuss in some depth was the meaning of the word 'work'. Did it have to be paid for it to be work? Was gardening work? Was cooking work? Was playing patience on my word processor when I am supposed to be writing a book work? Was the book itself work and how did writing it compare with, say, gardening? I took refuge in some line about the completion of a task, which reminded my wife that she hadn't completed dead-heading the roses. She was sure I wouldn't consider that was work.

At that moment the starters arrived. The goat cheese and pistachio soufflé got an ecstatic response, she had no idea it was such a good restaurant. My scallops were perfectly cooked, delicate and firm, with fresh samphire and very thin and very crisp pieces of bacon.

I think at that moment one of the tennis players was saying he either had or hadn't played Agassi, but my wife was back on the great debate. Was it work if you enjoyed doing it? Could talking be work? I said I thought it probably could.

For the main course she had calves' liver with grilled polenta and intense sauce which carried no supplement and was, from the bit I had and her more informed judgement, excellent. She was worried about the word "intense", which she thought might be slightly affected, but came to the conclusion it just meant "very reduced", and as gravy it was certainly as good as the thick chunks of liver, pink on the inside and very tender.

I had confit of duck with sage and olive oil mashed potato, which I was embarrassed to see did carry a supplement, this time of £2.50. There were plenty of alternatives without any surcharge, like fresh squid and prawns in a light curry sauce with risotto, or rabbit stifatho, or brochette of fresh Scotch salmon and monkfish with saffron tagliolini and sorrel sauce, and I suppose I should have had one of those, but the duck was wonderful and I am very glad I didn't. It fell off the bone, or off what little bone there was, the mashed potato with sage and olive oil was original and just right to go with it, and there was a side dish of carrot purée, new potatoes, red cabbage and broccoli, all of which could have come out of the garden that morning.

This, I am afraid, brought us back to the symposium. I rather foolishly suggested that work might be definable in terms of units of energy expended. My wife liked that idea and wondered whether it could be applied to what the lady in Hollywood did to

Hugh Grant. If that was work, would it have been work for anybody else?

The Hungry Monk's banoffi pudding has won awards, one of which is displayed as a blue plaque outside. I was offered a slice to taste and it is okay if you like toffee and banana. Instead I had tulipe – a sweet biscuit curled up at the sides – of lemon curd, crème fraîche and sorbet with fruit coulis, which I would put in a different league. The sorbet was blackcurrant and deserved a wallful of plaques to itself. My wife had a chocolate sponge pudding with toffee sauce. It was very, very, very good.

Dinner came to £68.04 without the tip. On the way out, my wife said she supposed that was what I called work.

John Wells

AFTER THE FREEDOM, BREAD

AT DAWN, the night train to Berlin would halt at the Griebnitzsee station. In the Cold War ages, this was the frontier post between East Germany and West Berlin. What used to wake me was not so much the wail of brakes and the jolt of the train stopping as the silence, the great enfolding silence which followed.

The passengers lay in their bunks, slipping in and out of dreams. Sometimes you heard the sound of jackboots marching along the platform outside and then fading away into the return of silence. Time ceased. Sometimes voices came from far off, somewhere down the train. Then more silence. I was always asleep again when the door finally flew open and a loud Saxon voice announced: 'Good morning. Your passports ...'

That timelessness, those tracts of utter silence inhabited by dreams, seems to me now to have been the essence of the Cold War. History had stopped, history was waiting. This pause, which had already lasted for most of my adult lifetime, was apparently set to last for ever. And yet the Griebnitzsee dreams were always uneasy. In the silence, denser when the long, empty, forbidden platforms were carpeted with snow, things were building up. New generations were being born and leaving school, both in East and West, understanding their world in new ways, the mass of their hopes and frustrations accumulating every day. At the heart of the silence, the needle of a pressure gauge was creeping round towards explosion.

Five years ago, the pressure broke through. Since then, Europe has been full of noise and tumult, without time for dreams. This tumult is not exactly the 'result' of the 1989 revolutions. Instead, it is the torrential outrush – still not subsiding – of all the forces of history that were pent up for nearly half a century. The revolutions, brave and glorious as they were, did not so much puncture the Communist systems as find leaks and instantly enlarge then into gaping, irreparable rents.

The Berlin Wall fell five years ago last week; the Prague revolution's anniversary comes in a few days. But in Poland, which had been leading the whole process since 1980, a government led by anti-Communists had already taken office in September, while the new Hungarian Republic, formally opening the door to 'bourgeois democracy', had been proclaimed in October. Most of this was brought about by clever, courageous, young men and women possessed by the Zeitgeist and hardened by years of underground conspiracy. They seized the moment to push weak governments into round-table talks, or to call people on to the streets. They changed the world, and gave to millions of fellow-citizens the most brilliantly happy few days of their lives.

Hindsight does not lessen what they did, in Wenceslas Square or on the streets of Leipzig and Budapest, but it broadens the background. What happened in 1989 was one consequence of great changes in the whole European environment.

The 'Golden Years', the colossal increase in prosperity

and living standards which lasted from about 1950 to the early 1970s, dumped most of their blessings in the West. But the wealth and the growth also overflowed to strengthen and even stabilise the Communist regimes of the East. When the boom broke, however, the West proved able to cope with the long recession that followed, while the East could not.

During the good years, many Communist states had – in varying degrees – opened their economies to the West. Now they were landed with contracting markets, soaring foreign debts and imported inflation. Their inflexible systems could not adapt. The computer revolution – part of the West's response to the 1970s crisis – was too expensive to import, and the technology gap between East and West began to widen disastrously.

At home, regimes faced growing unrest from populations tormented by spreading shortages, queueing and frustrated expectations. By 1980, the hopeless failure of Soviet-model Communism not just as a political creed but as a system of production and distribution was clear to everyone.

Some reformers thought that a 'liberalised' national Communism could close the gap again. The majority, those with no voice, suspected that Communism was unreformable.

Soon a 'Catch '89' became apparent. No radical reform of Communism could be tried until the threat of Soviet armed intervention was lifted, but at the same time it was increasingly obvious that it was only that threat which kept any form of Communist regime going, reformed or otherwise. When Mikhail Gorbachev did cautiously and elliptically withdraw the implied menace (the old 'Brezhnev Doctrine') in the 1980s, it was too late for any change short of revolution.

In that strange interval between the overthrow of the Wall and the unification of Germany in 1990, it seemed for a time as if a separate East Germany might survive as a new model of plural, democratic socialism. People who wanted this spoke of it, unwisely, as a noble experiment. But the East German voters recoiled. They had suffered too much as the guinea-pigs of one sort of political experiment to risk another. Capitalism, on the other hand, was not an experiment. In the West it worked. We'll have that, they said. Millions of people all over the collapsing Soviet empire felt the same.

What they actually got was another experiment: as wild and ideological, in its first years, as the imposition of Soviet Communism. All over East-Central Europe and Russia dashed the young missionaries of an extreme, Thatcherite version of the free-market economy – a version so radical and ruthless that no Western electorate would have tolerated it for a moment. Not everything about that onslaught was wrong. The Polish economy went straight over Niagara in a barrel, abolishing retail subsidies and cutting the currency loose to find its own level – and survived. But the next stage – trying to cancel all industrial subsidies so that every factory not in profit went instantly bankrupt – would have wrecked the country if it had been carried through.

As it was, the free-market experiment in eastern Europe set off a terrifying race. Could a market economy get installed and start spreading wealth before the agonies of transition – crashing living standards, mass unemployment – destroyed public confidence in democratic governments? Luckily, this race has been called off before the last lap. The pace of change has been slowed; privatisation goes ahead cautiously; no-hope industries with enormous no-hope workforces are treated gingerly, and the state pays to make their death gradual and painless. The Thatcherites are mostly out of the ministries and running private consultancies. The governments which employed them in Poland and Hungary have been replaced by coalitions around reformed post-Communist parties. In the Czech Republic, Vaclav Klaus talks free-market rhetoric but uses his budget to keep uneconomic industries in work.

The Polish writer Aleksander Smolar, reviewing the past five years, sees three kinds of politician: moderates, radicals and counter-revolutionaries. The moderates are liberal anti-Communists who led the revolutions and founded the market economies. The radicals are right-wingers, usually fanatical nationalists and ultra-conservatives, who want to purge the nation of Communists, Jews and foreigners. The counter-revolutionaries are reformed post-Communists – Smolar calls them the 'Old-New' people – who would like to restore the old regime without its faults.

But, here again, both parts of Europe are really marching in the same direction at different paces. In the West, the economic crisis of the 1970s drove many governments to adopt extreme free-market policies in a vain attempt to revive the steady growth of the 'Golden Years'. When they failed, as Thatcherism failed in this country when a new storm of recession hit the world in the late 1980s, there began a drift back towards the politics of centrism and consensus.

Post-Communist Europe has simply compressed this process, whizzing through it in five years rather than 15. The mood which has persuaded millions of people in Poland, Hungary and eastern Germany to vote for the neo-Communists – a turn as unexpected as the 1989 revolutions themselves – is the same mood which is tugging Western public opinion back towards the ideal of a state which guides and restrains market forces. Smolar's 'Old-New' reformed Communists have at least something in common with Tony Blair's 'New Labour Party'. Both think they can restore what was good about the ancien regime before the revolution, and leave its unaccept-

able bits behind. Both believe, in Eric Hobsbawm's words, that 'the economic miracles [of the 20th century] were not achieved by laissez-faire but against it'.

When the Wall fell, it seemed that a divided Europe was being put together again. The barbed wire was uprooted; the bridges, cleared of weeds and barricades, reopened for traffic. But in reality a 'united' Europe has never existed before, apart from brief and ghastly experiments under Napoleon and Hitler. That lost 'Europe without passports' is a nostalgic myth; it was true only sometimes in some western parts of the continent and then only for the rich. So is it not more 'natural' that Europe – after a few merry years – should revert to its normal condition of being divided?

The first post-'89 fear was that a free-market Europe would split into 'metropolis' and 'colonies'. The West would have all the money and industry. In the East, there would be total deindustrialisation as the state economies collapsed, and eastern Europe would revert to a peasant backwater supplying the West with fruit, vegetables, raw materials and cheap labour.

This is not going to happen. The combination of highly trained work forces, low wages and foreign investment is already bringing industrial recovery in eastern Europe. At least three post-Communist states (Poland, Hungary and the Czech Republic) will probably be inside the European

Union by the end of the century. And yet the danger of a new partition, a new Iron Curtain, still exists.

This is the security problem – the enigma of Russia's future. Who, for example, will guarantee the independence of the Baltic states? If Nato eventually takes them in, Russia and her clients in the Confederation of Independent States may wall themselves off again. What space would then remain between the two re-emerging blocs for the independence of Bulgaria or Romania, and what would be the options for Serbia? The Cold War managed to bury and forget the true European riddle which is only now resurfacing: our Europe ends at the Atlantic, but where does it begin?

This has been a low-key fifth anniversary for the revolutions. The exultation of those days – what the poet Erich Fried called 'the happiness of the hope of happiness' – is only a memory. People talk readily of disillusion, of cultural collapse, of brutal acquisitiveness and tribal intolerance. Those who led the revolutions and often the first free governments, the 'Forum' people with their liberal and international ideals, their battle honours in devoted opposition, their brilliant intelligence – they have been swept away.

They were amateurs at politics. Now the professionals, mediocre and cunning, have taken over. The 'social democrats', the renamed ex-Communists, have revived partly because the populations are sick of unemployment but also – just as important – because they offer a sort of absolution to those millions who declined to be heroes and made their own compromises with the Communist regimes. For pessimists, it can seem that all the gains of 1989 are running away into the sand, leaving most people more demoralised than they were before. Ahead lies a cynical, 'Italianised' form of society, in which 'they pretend to govern, and we pretend to pay taxes'.

In 1989, I read a Solidarity election poster nailed to the door of an ancient wooden church. It began with these words: 'Look at Europe and the world. Where is there most bread and freedom? There is most bread and freedom in those states whose peoples in free elections choose their own rulers, to make the laws and form governments and parliaments . . .'

In the post-Communist lands, once again responding to a general European current, there is a broad disgust with parties and politicians. Their world seems to have lost touch with the 'real' world of the needs and choices of ordinary people. And yet the disgust is with the structure of democratic politics as it exists, with the squabbling knot of foremen in the ugly building site that is eastern Europe today. The hope of a better politics is not dead. The simple statement on that poster – that bread, liberty and democracy belong together – is not disputed.

After an experience like 1989, a hangover was to be expected. President Vaclav Havel calls it the 'post-prison syndrome'; the Hungarian writer George Konrad refers to 'the melancholy of rebirth'. And yet these may be remembered as triumphant years. Some triumphs were positive, like the wild-horse economic strength displayed by these societies – supposedly stripped of initiative by Communism. Some were negative, like all the minority problems which did not explode because they were handled sensibly for the first time in history. The great transformation could have been done less wastefully and callously, doing more to protect the people and less to enrich gangsters. But it is working. The bread is at last beginning to arrive, a long time after the freedom.

Neal Ascherson
13.11.94

Photographs

Picture A – Girl's face behind a window

Picture B – Woman sitting on railway bench

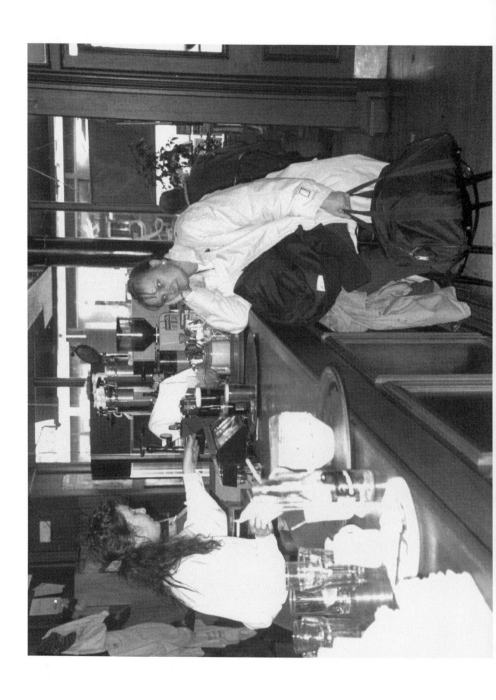

Picture C – Woman 'alone' in pub with suitcase

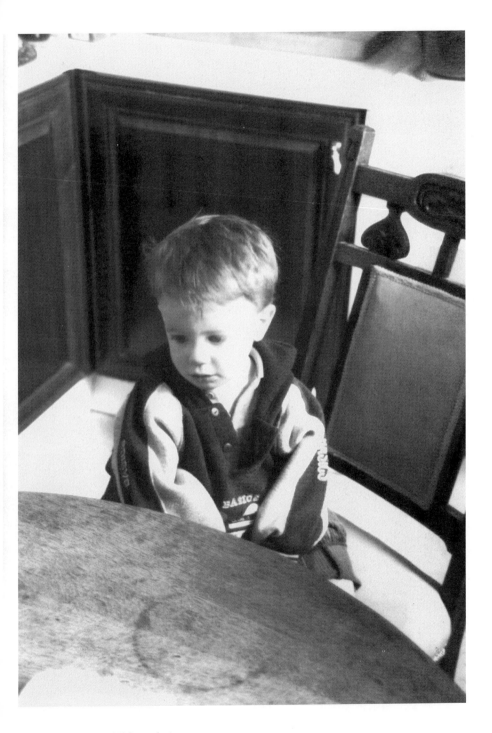

Picture D – Young child on chair

Picture E – Man and a woman and street poster

Picture F – Corner of derelict building

Picture G – Homelessness   (© Angus Boulton)

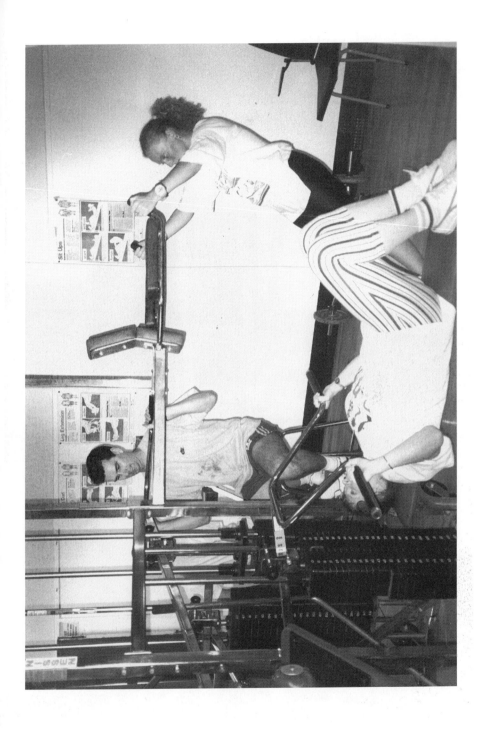

Picture H – Keep-fit scene in gym

Further Photographs

The photographs on pages 128–133 may stimulate further creative writing.

In the News

New heart warning for smokers

The Herald

Heart attack in younger smokers 'five times more likely'

The Guardian

Heart attack risk 6 times bigger for young smokers

The Daily Telegraph

Doctors revise smokers' heart risk

The Scotsman

Risk of heart attack five times higher for middle-aged smoker

The Times

Tories deflated as Blair revolt turns into farce

The Guardian, front page

Patrick Wintour, Chief Political Correspondent

THE Conservative assault on Tony Blair was left badly punctured last night when one of the most damaging criticisms of his leadership style, an unrestrained assault supposedly by the former shadow cabinet minister, Bryan Gould, proved to have been written by the teenage son of the Home Secretary, Michael Howard.

The near-farcical news deflated Conservative Central Office and left crimson faces at the Evening Standard, the London newspaper which printed, under the name of Mr Gould, the attack on Mr Blair written by 19-year-old Nick Howard.

'Gould' attack on Blair written by Home Secretary's son

The Scotsman, front page

By Joy Copley

A VICIOUS attack on Tony Blair carried under the name of Bryan Gould, the former shadow cabinet member, in the London *Evening Standard*, was in fact written by the son of the Home Secretary, Michael Howard.

The remarkable mistake came to light after Mr Gould, who lives in New Zealand, was faxed a copy of the article, which has been used all week as a stick to beat the Labour leader.

The *Evening Standard* started an inquiry and said that, as a result of a series of errors and by "extraordinary mischance", it had published the wrong article.

Apology to Gould as paper gets fax wrong

The Daily Telegraph, front page

IN ONE of the most abject apologies in the annals of Fleet Street, a newspaper admitted yesterday that a withering attack on Tony Blair that appeared under the name of a former Shadow Cabinet colleague was in fact written by the 19-year-old son of a Tory minister.

The London *Evening Standard* blamed "an extraordinary series of mishaps" for its mistake in publishing, under the by-line of Bryan Gould, an article actually written by Nick Howard, the student son of Michael Howard, the Home Secretary.

The article's criticism of the Labour leader as "solely interested in power" and likely to face "massive divisions among MPs and members" in government fuelled the row over Mr Blair's style of management and gave valuable ammunition to Tory claims of a growing mutiny.

135

Gould not behind attack on Blair

Daily Mail, page 2

A NEWSPAPER article attacking Tony Blair – which appeared under the name of former Shadow Cabinet member Bryan Gould – was not written by him at all, it emerged yesterday.

The Evening Standard said that as a result of a series of errors and by 'extraordinary mischance' it had published the wrong article in its Monday editions.

The remarks attributed to Mr Gould were reported in good faith, and commented on, by the Daily Mail and most other newspapers.

Newspaper gaffe spares Blair embarrassment

The Times, front page

BY **ALAN HAMILTON**

TONY BLAIR returns to London tomorrow to face the task of trying to silence Labour critics who have accused him of riding roughshod over the views of party members. But he will be spared one embarrassing issue, at least.

The London *Evening Standard* yesterday apologised for running a widely quoted article attributed to Bryan Gould, the former Shadow Cabinet member, criticising Mr Blair's style of leadership. But the article was apparently by Nicholas Howard, 19, the aspiring journalist son of Michael Howard, the Home Secretary.

Own Gould .. attack on Blair gets its fax wrong

Daily Mirror, page 2

Gould row was fax-up

The Sun, page 2

An article slamming Tony Blair under the name of ex-Labour bigwig Bryan Gould was, in fact, written by Home Secretary Michael Howard's son Nick. London Evening Standard editor Stewart Steven blamed a fax error.

Index